Road Trip

A Love Letter to America

Sharon Canfield Dorsey

HighTide
Publications, Inc.

Deltaville, Virginia

High Tide Publications, Inc.

Deltaville, Virginia 23043

www.HighTidePublications.com

Edited by Linda Partee and Cindy L. Freeman

Photographs by Don Frew

Printed in the United States of America

ISBN: 978-1945990861

Contents

What readers like you are saying about *Road Trip:*

CARLTON HARDY...

Reading *Road Trip* is like having coffee with a dear friend. Sharon's first-person commentary on touristy spots as well as those roads less traveled breathes life into them. The author has a facility with words and a perspective of people, places and history that draws you into her journeys. Her historical notes and background comments give vibrancy to her stories. Her personal connection to the places, history, and the plight of Native Americans lends further credence to her writing. These memories of travels with her husband/best friend, Don, provide glimpses into the soul of places seldom seen, including finding the positive aspects of grit on a hotel dining room table in Jerome, Arizona.

CHRIS TINGLE...

This was a delightful read. *Road Trip* offers factual information, as do all travel books, but above all, it is fun! The personal notations about the places visited create a spectacular imagery that make the reader eager to hit the road in hopes of experiencing the same back roads, locals and events as the author.

CINDY FREEMAN...

What a stunning book! It is beautifully written and the author's Native American spirit shines through every page. You will want to read this book again and again. I do!

ED LULL...

Sharon Dorsey's *Road Trip* is filled with travel adventures most of us only dream of, and the impact those adventures have on the human spirit. In exploring her Native American heritage, she records a moving poem, Being Indian, and the Algonquin Code of Ethics. Her explorations of Alaska and Hawaii are riveting, as are her scary moments, such as being robbed at gunpoint and her edge-of-the-cliff experience at the Grand Canyon. This is a fine literary work filled with excellent writing, great photography and research. This is a book you will read more than once!

VIVIEN MANN...

This book is truly captivating. *Road Trip* is a lovely mix of creative sharing and great travel tips. It is a true love letter to America!

ANN SHALASKI...

I took advantage of a quiet Sunday to fall in love with *Road Trip*, wishing I was the traveler. See, through Sharon Canfield Dorsey's travel journal, a romance filled with endless treasures spread far and wide, shared with the light of her life. Live, love, and learn with Sharon and Don. This little gem tugs at your heartstrings. It's as inviting and enriching as hot chocolate in December.

KAYE LEVY...

Most of my life traveling has been done overseas. *Road Trip* has inspired me to want to visit the places described and more, here in our country. This book has just the right amount of factual information paired with emotional responses to the places visited. Makes me want to pack my bags and hit the road.

If you enjoyed *Road Trip*, please consider leaving a review on Amazon.com. Amazon accepts reviews from readers even if they did not purchase the book on Amazon. Sign in under your Amazon account, enter *Road Trip Sharon Dorsey* in the search block to find her book. You can add a review when the Amazon page with *Road Trip* appears on your screen. Thank you so much for supporting our authors.

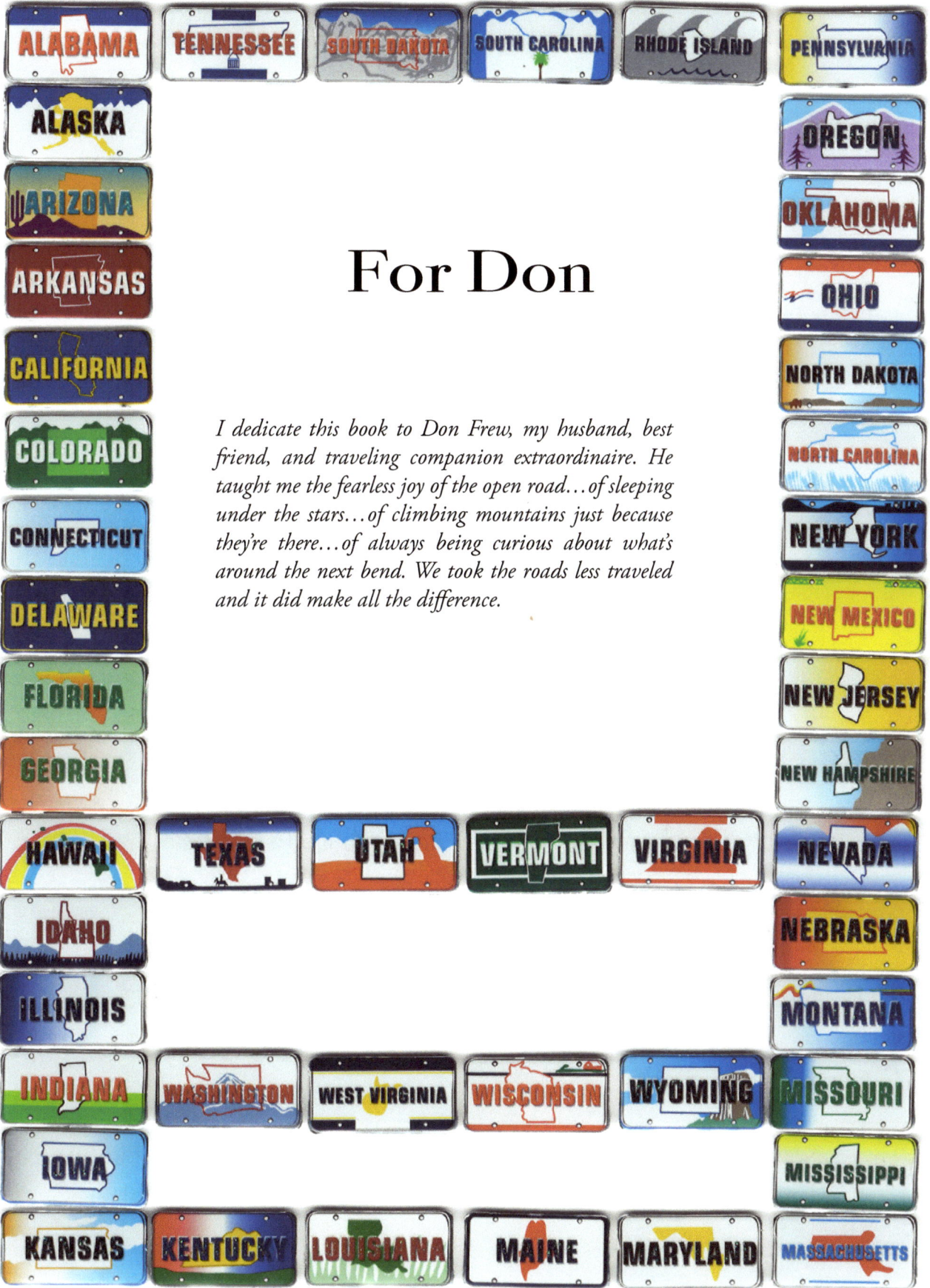

For Don

I dedicate this book to Don Frew, my husband, best friend, and traveling companion extraordinaire. He taught me the fearless joy of the open road…of sleeping under the stars…of climbing mountains just because they're there…of always being curious about what's around the next bend. We took the roads less traveled and it did make all the difference.

Road Trip...A Travel Memoir

I thought it would be a fun project to do,
some stories to tell, a short poem or two.
A travel memoir, I thought I might call it.
It grew and it grew...now I can't halt it.

We flew to Hawaii, explored every island.
I wanted to stay there, watch sunsets and get tanned.
We drove to Alaska and camped in the Yukon;
panned gold in old Skagway, the miners are long gone.

We drove east and west, then north and south.
So many great places. Can't sort them all out.
I saw an old postcard one day in a store —
a sun-bonneted lady, doing her chores.

She bent over a fire by a Conestoga wagon.
She was stirrin' the stew, all energy laggin'.
The caption said just what I wanted to say,
"Been traveling a lot. Ate out again today."

Chapter 1

Road Trip

A Love Letter to America

How We Caught The Travel Bug

When my husband, Don, retired from the Air Force, he was eager to explore America – its mountains, its rivers, its "off the beaten path" small towns. When I met him, he was already a skier, hiker and an experienced kayaker. I, on the other hand, liked to write and read books. That could have spelled a quick end to this "second time around" romance. But I was a willing student. Taking a deep breath, I decided to embrace the adventure. It's one of the best decisions I ever made.

Florida

Our "his and hers" children were grown, so we began our travels together by going to visit them. But we didn't just sit around their houses. We researched each area to find out what fun things we could do there. My daughter, Shannon, lived in Florida for several years. We played in Disney World, Sea World, Splendid China, Universal Studios…the list goes on. We explored botanical gardens, quirky museums, and knew where every upscale thrift store was in Palm Beach.

On a trip to Key West, we went in search of "Amy's Secret Garden," hidden away in the middle of a busy business district. We had read about it in one of our travel books. Over a period of years, a talented naturalist had completely surrounded her home with a dense rain-forest-type vegetation, and populated it with rainbow-hued parrots and macaws who were happy to perch on your shoulder for a handful of seed. Don said it made him feel like a pirate. The Secret Garden more than lived up to its reviews.

Kentucky

Because we both loved to read, we collected travel books which became dog-eared and sometimes stained with peanut butter, Don's favorite travel food. It was like a scavenger hunt in every new city, to find the places we'd read about. When my son, Steven, moved to Kentucky, we could hardly wait to visit the rolling hills and elaborate horse farms near his new home in Versailles. We learned that Mammoth Caves National Park was nearby, so as soon as son and daughter-in-law were off to work each morning, we were off exploring. We also learned that Versailles had interesting antique stores on every corner. None was safe from us. Do you sense an underlying shopping agenda here?

Outer Banks, N. C.

Don's son, Greg, owned a beach house in the Outer Banks of North Carolina but lived in New York most of the time, so we did our best to keep that empty house from feeling lonely.

We became avid beachcombers, carrying home seashell treasures and using maps to search for sunken ships, buried in the sand along the ocean shore. We loved going there after a big storm when the seas had done the work for us, uncovering old timbers from those lost ships. We explored lighthouses up and down that stretch of coastline and bravely fought off mosquitoes in nature areas to spy on birds and wildlife. When the Cape Hatteras Lighthouse, circa. 1870, was moved back 2,900 feet from the edge of the sea because of the threat of erosion, we were there to see the whole incredible project unfold. The spectacle of the tallest lighthouse in the United States – a 4,830-ton brick structure – moving along steel rails, an inch at a time, to its new home base was a never-to-be-forgotten sight.

New York City

One of our driving trips was up the East Coast, from Virginia to Maine. Although we were happiest in jeans and t-shirts, we pulled out our "fancy" dress for a detour to New York City and several nights at the theatre. During the days, we wandered through as many museums as possible, also paying a visit to Lady Liberty. I insisted on riding the subway, ONCE. We agreed the George Gustav Heye Museum of the American Indian was our favorite. Don had an interest in Indian culture because he spent his boyhood summers in Albuquerque, N. M., hiking in the hills among the petroglyphs. My interest came from wanting to know more about my native heritage. Years after our visit to N. Y., we would be privileged to attend the opening of the National Museum of the American Indian in Washington, D. C.

When we left the confines of New York City and headed north to New England, we both drew a sigh of relief. You can take the people out of the country but…well, you know how that goes. We were happy to be back in our jeans and t-shirts.

New England

We fell in love with New England. I ordered my first lobster at a charming little café by the sea in Cape Cod. Unfortunately, I left it in that same charming café. It was those eyes staring at me! The chef was understanding. He removed the lobster and created a delicious vegetarian pasta for me. It was one of those on-the-road lessons.

One day, in Vermont, we followed a sign advertising maple syrup and found ourselves on a dirt road, too narrow for turn-arounds, that seemed to go on forever. After nearly an hour, the road dead-ended at a deserted-looking farm with ramshackle barns and out-buildings. Disappointed, we were turning around to leave when a smiling Santa Claus look-alike appeared. He had a wonderful Norwegian accent and gave us a tour of the farm, throwing in a visit to the horse barns. Inside one rickety barn was a spotless, stainless steel syrup-making operation. We brought home maple syrup for everyone we knew.

It sounds like a cliché to say that New England's mountains are stunning in the fall, but they are – a tapestry of scarlets and golds stretching for miles. We were lucky to be there at just the right time.

West Virginia

On the trip back to Virginia, we stopped in my hometown of Charmco, West Virginia to visit my mother. I had never really thought about sight-seeing in my hometown but it wasn't Don's hometown and he'd done his research, so off we went in search of a new adventure. My father was a coal miner and I grew up in Appalachian coal country but I had never gone down into a coal mine. As the chill of that dim cavern closed in around me and the rattling, squealing coal cars carried us deep underground, I found myself tearing up at the thought of the days, months and years my dad spent in this other-worldly, dark, damp, hell hole. He survived to retire but with damaged knees, a stooped back and Black Lung. Many of his friends weren't even that lucky. Cave-ins were common in those days of NO mining regulations. They took the lives of many friends and family.

To counteract the gloom of the mine, I insisted on equal time. TAMARAC is a unique cultural center, near Beckley, West Virginia, showcasing local artisans from all around the state. You can peruse every kind of art, from paintings to coal carvings and everything in between. The Center also features "The Best of West Virginia Restaurant," with such local delicacies as Fried Green Tomatoes, West Virginia Rainbow Trout, and Greenbrier Peach Cobbler.

north entrance to the Greenbrier gives no clues to a secret bunker for Congress.
tesy of The Greenbrier Resort

Visit To A Secret Bunker

At one time, the historic Greenbrier Resort in White Sulphur Springs, West Virginia, circa 1778, was a front for a secret 112,544 sq. ft. bunker to protect members of Congress in case of nuclear attack or other threats. Locals knew about it because many of them worked on the construction of the shelter, which was dug 720 feet into the mountain. We heard it had a 25-ton blast door, decontamination chambers, 18 dormitories accommodating over 1,100 people, a power plant and water storage tanks. We didn't know it had four entrances, housed a clinic with 12 hospital beds and operating rooms, a communications area for television production and recording, a laboratory and pharmacy, cafeteria, and completely equipped meeting rooms for the House and Senate.

In the Greenbrier's public exhibition hall, a not-so-secret entrance leads to the bunker.
Guy Raz/NPR

It was an active facility from 1961 to 1992, kept at full operational status. On May 31, 1992, the Washington Post published an article that exposed the facility. With it's cover blown, the U. S Government was forced to decommission The Bunker. Tours are now offered to hotel guests and the general public. It is an awesome sight.

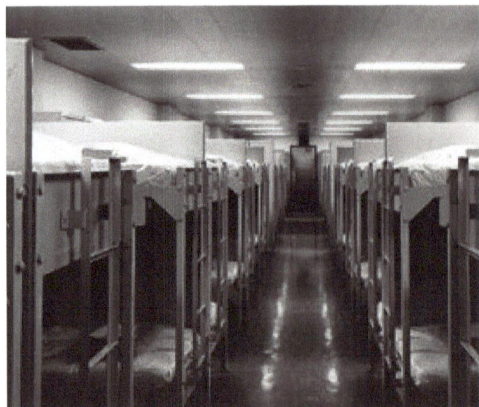

Beds line the dormitory for members of Congress.
Courtesy of The Greenbrier

A Cautionary Tale

It was dusk when we decided to stop for the night on our journey back to Williamsburg from a Florida visit with my daughter, Shannon. We knew the going-home traffic through Savanna, Georgia would be bumper to bumper so we chose a hotel on the outskirts, just off the interstate and decided to call it a day. We traveled a lot and knew all the stories about seniors being targets for robbers so we were overly cautious, always staying in hotels or motels where we could park outside our room and never leaving anything in the back seat to tempt a thief.

Don checked us into a room on the first floor, beside the lobby entrance. We always traveled with too much stuff and this trip was no exception. Besides the usual clothes, books, etc., we were also returning with Christmas presents. I carried in the first load from the back seat, turned around to go back for another and was stopped by a black man in a hoodie in the doorway, pointing a gun at me. Before I could think, another man entered the room with Don, holding a gun to his head and shouting, "Don't anybody move!" My heart jumped into my throat.

My first thought was, "Please Don, don't try to be a hero." I was afraid his years of combat training would kick in and he would try to take them down. But he didn't. He was very calm, almost friendly. He pulled out his wallet, opened it and began pulling out money and credit cards. "There's over $400 here. Could I keep the wallet? It has my kids pictures in it." I remember thinking, "What a weird thing to say when you're about to be shot." The man lowered the gun from Don's head, shoved him over beside me, took the money and cards, leaving the wallet in Don's hand. My purse was on my shoulder. I slid it down my arm and held it out to the man holding the gun on me, not saying a word. I wasn't brave enough to bargain. He took it and pushed both of us into the bathroom, slamming the door and yelling, "Don't come out or you're dead!"

We heard a lot of commotion, yelling back and forth, and what sounded like the phone being thrown to the floor. Don pulled me away from the door, pointed to the bathtub and we both crawled in, Don's body over mine, protecting me. Later, Don told me he thought they might shoot through the door and that seemed the safest place. We waited for what seemed an eternity. My mind was blank. It was as if something had turned off all emotion, including fear. Much later, when I revisited those moments, I wondered if that's how people feel when their plane is going down, if our minds somehow protect us from the horror of what is happening to us by sending us into shock. In some strange way, I've always been comforted by that thought.

Eventually, we heard the door slam but we didn't move for the longest time. Don crawled out of the bathtub, finally, and opened the door a crack. The room was empty but we still didn't dare leave the bathroom because we were afraid they'd come back. We waited and waited till we heard car doors slam outside and what sounded like a vehicle screeching out of the parking lot. Still, we waited. Don cautiously opened the bathroom door and I watched him crawl over to the telephone on the floor. Thank goodness, it still worked. Oh yeah, I should have mentioned, this was before we had cell phones.

He called the lobby and almost instantly, someone was banging on the door. "Open up! It's safe! I've called the cops." Still suspicious, Don pulled the curtain back an inch and peeped out. He recognized the desk clerk and opened the door. Moments later, sirens ushered in two police cars and we felt safe enough to step outside. All four doors of our car and the trunk were open. All had been ransacked, suitcases opened and stuff strewn about, some on the ground.

The police wouldn't let us touch anything. One of them started dusting the doors for fingerprints. The other one escorted us into the lobby to take our statements. He also questioned the clerk about security cameras and asked to see the footage. Ironically, all the cameras were working except the one on that corner of the building. Later, when everything was finished, we asked the officer what the chances were of catching the robbers.

He shook his head, "Practically none. We'll put all the information into the system and see if anyone comes up but this is the third hotel robbery in the area this week. There's a gang that targets the hotels near the interstate. We haven't been able to catch them. The interstate makes escape easy. They just move on to the next hotel. They're looking for guns, drugs and cash, nothing easily traced." When we walked outside, he continued, "We feel sure the robbers have accomplices in the hotels who disable the cameras but we haven't been able to prove it. I'm so sorry you were victimized. I searched all the outside trash cans, hoping we could find your discarded purse, but no luck."

When the police went on their way, the hotel manager continued to apologize, offering a complimentary room in a different part of the hotel. We looked at each other and shook our heads. We just wanted out of there. But there were practical issues. We had no money and no credit cards and we were many hours away from home. The hotel gave us $100 cash, acting as if they were performing a great service. Don used the lobby phone to call an Army base that was about 100 miles away, explained our problem, including how traumatized we were and that we needed to be someplace where we felt safe. They assured us a room would be waiting.

On the drive there, I learned why Don had tried to hold on to his wallet, aside from saving his driver's license. He always carried a list of our credit cards along with a check, folded up and hidden in the wallet. We would be able to call and cancel the cards, then cash the check for enough money to get home. When we arrived at Ft. Jackson, a room was waiting in the VIP quarters. An MP escorted us to our room. He even helped us unload the car so we could repack the belongings that we had just piled in the trunk as we beat our hasty retreat. To our surprise, the robbers didn't take anything from the car, not even my jewelry.

There wasn't much sleeping the rest of that night. We called the credit card companies, reassured ourselves that all of our things were there, repacked them and dropped into bed as the sun was coming up. We awakened in time for lunch, cashed our only check, refueled the car, and headed home.

Epilogue

They didn't catch the robbers, to nobody's surprise. Our insurance covered the money that was stolen. It even covered the roll of fifty Regal movie tickets my son-in-law, a theatre manager, had given me for Christmas. We continued to stay in hotels on our car trips without any other scary occurrence.

Lesson Re-Learned

Never leave home without a check, a list of your credit cards and an extra car key in some clever hiding place in your vehicle.

Road Trip

A Love Letter to America

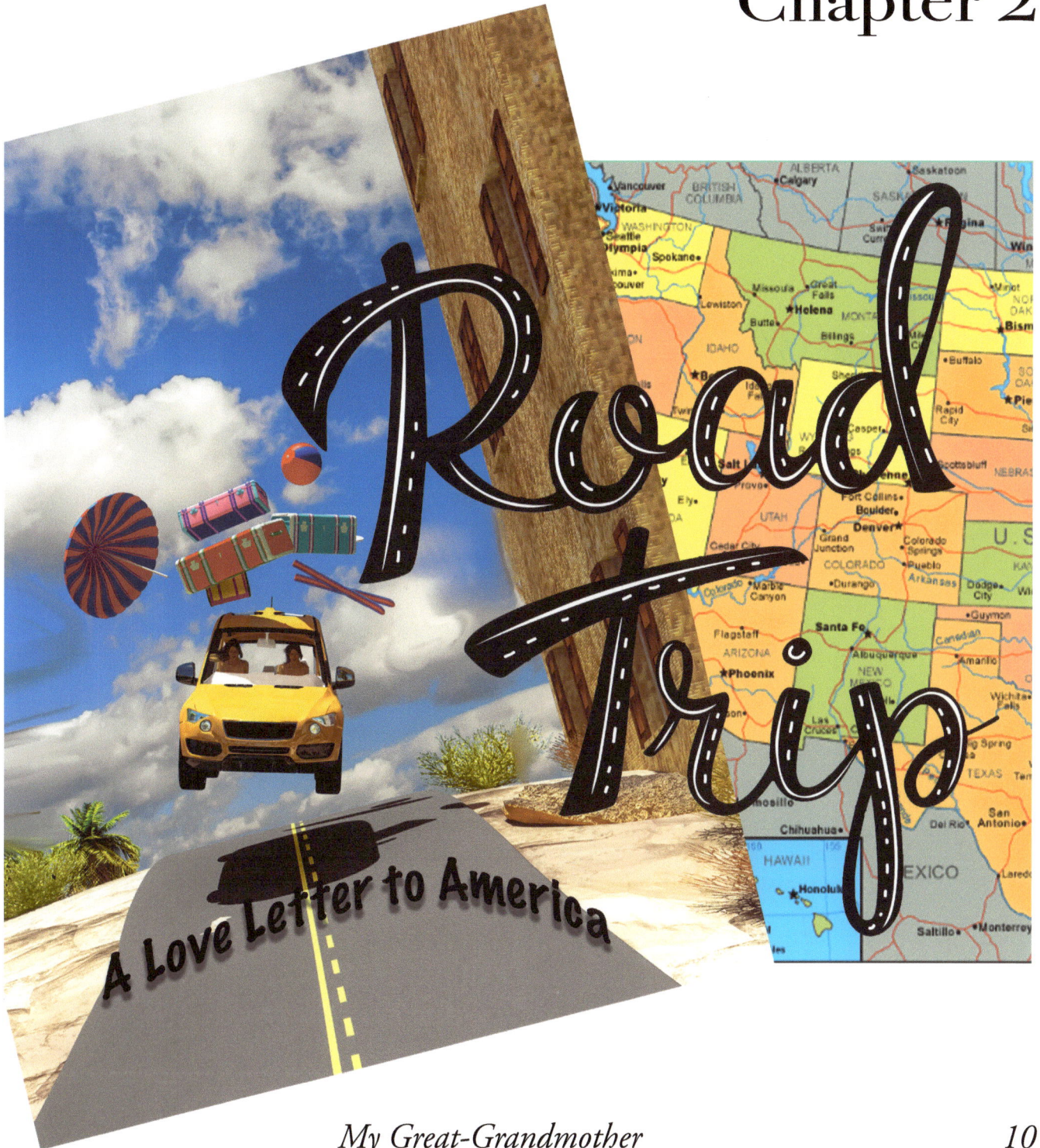

Sharon Canfield Dorsey

My Great-Grandmother

I wish I knew her story,
my great-grandmother, Martha.
She was Indian, full-blooded Cherokee,
who migrated to the Appalachian Mountains.

She married William, my great-grandfather,
a farmer, son of an Irish immigrant,
who had divided his farm land among his sons.
William and Martha raised five children together.

I study her photograph,
the high cheekbones,
the dark, straight hair,
the inscrutable staring eyes.

As a child, I was told I looked like her,
but nobody told me her story.
How and when did her family find their way
from North Carolina to West Virginia?

Did they escape from the infamous Trail of Tears?
Between four and eight thousand Cherokee died on that march.
She would have been ten years old at the beginning of the relocation
of sixteen thousand Indians from North Carolina to Oklahoma.

How terrified a ten-year-old would have been,
to be ripped from her home,
stripped of her possessions,
then watch it all go up in flames.

I located her name on the Cherokee identity rolls.
I have a faded copy of her tintype photograph.
I know she was born in 1828.

I wish, oh, how I wish, I knew the rest of her story.

10

Being Indian

Fire shadows give motion to figures etched on stone.
Escaping spirits shimmer and dance in the firelight
as I dream of lives long past.

Being Indian is not just a percentage of bloodline.
It is a feeling in your heart
connecting you to Mother Earth, to the ancestors.

It is sitting beneath an ancient oak,
listening to the wind whisper to the leaves,
thanking the Great Spirit for his blessings.

It's marveling at the grandeur of a canyon,
the quiet whir of tiny hummingbird wings,
lightning dancing across a darkening summer sky.

It's shedding tears for concrete landscapes,
polluted air, and plastic-filled oceans.
Maybe that's not just being Indian.

Maybe that's being human.

Sharon Canfield Dorsey

Belonging To Mother Earth

During one of our "home in Virginia" periods, we learned about a conference in Virginia Beach that was bringing together an extraordinary group of Native American and indigenous spiritual leaders from all over the world. The purpose of the "Belonging to Mother Earth Conference" was to remind us of our responsibility to care for the earth, our home, and to discuss solutions for the problems we have brought upon ourselves and our planet. Don and I are avid environmentalists and this was an opportunity we couldn't pass up. We had no way of knowing this week would enlighten and broaden our lives in so many ways.

Hand-painted banners wave in the grassy area in front of the conference hotel. A campfire burns nearby, tended by moccasined men and women. The scent of sage and sweet grass fills the air. The plaintive notes of a flute can be heard in the distance while the slow heartbeat of a drum pounds out the rhythm of a chant.

We watch in awe that first night as these spiritual pilgrims gather…creating a unique tapestry of languages, cultures and histories, bringing with them hopes of peace and dreams of healing the earth, our Mother, and perhaps, in the process, healing themselves.

Resplendent in fringed deerskin, gleaming silks and colorful embroideries, they cross the stage, announcing their tribal affiliation…Eastern Cherokee, the tribe of my ancestors, the Mattaponi, Lakota, Hopi, Blackfoot, Western Shoshone, Choctaw the list goes on, all tribes of Turtle Island, the Indian name for America. They are joined by their global sisters and brothers from Argentina, Panama, El Salvador, Peru, Chile, Guatemala, Costa Rica, Senegal, Caribbean, Canada, New Zealand, West Africa, Siberia, some speaking English, some making introductions in their native tongue. Most of these nations are together under the same roof for the first time. There will be many questions of protocol during the week. There will be times when it will be difficult to set aside old grievances. But tonight, all agree it is a time of rebuilding - of holding fast to tradition while moving ahead into the future. It is a time for re-emergence of native peoples around the globe, a time to teach and a time to lead. All express concern about the opposing values in our society, particularly the difficult questions of money versus clean air and water and the preservation of wild places.

The first evening ends with an Ojibway prayer:

Grandfather, look at our brokenness. We know that in all creation, only the human family has strayed from the Sacred Way. We know that we are the ones who are divided, and we are the ones who must come back together to walk in the Sacred Way. Grandfather, Sacred One, teach us love, compassion, and honor that we may heal the Earth and heal each other.

During our week, there are moments of revelation. A Cherokee grandmother speaks of ancient prophesies promising the rebirth of the nations and tribes of the world to preeminence. To a hushed room, she declares,

We are the Ancient Ones. We have returned to help cleanse the earth.

In other gatherings, we listen to the Siberians lament the fact that their homeland is being mined for the first time. The tracings left behind are bringing disease to a people who have been the longest living citizens on earth.

We are moved by the frustrations of the Incas, who are, every day, losing more precious rain forest. Their healers are certain the cures for cancer and other diseases are to be found there, but they fear they cannot work fast enough to outrun the chainsaws.

We hear the former president of Costa Rica lament that large drug companies are coming into his country, stealing the remedies that have been passed down from centuries of healers, and patenting them, so his people cannot even use them for their own families.

We grieve with the Native American tribes as they describe the difficulty of sustaining their families on land that is some of the worst and most useless in this country and is now being used for dumping grounds for nuclear waste.

There are small victories...

...finding a volunteer who will donate a special computer program to a Siberian doctor who needs it for his cancer research and was unable to obtain it at home.

...a helping hand, termed simply, Coats Across America, evolves from one of our discussion circles, when we learn of elderly Native Americans who need warm clothing in the winter. It was simple. We all have extras. They need them, so we will send them. Done!

One day, an Algonquin grandfather shares with us a memorable native Code of Ethics:

1. Each morning, when you wake up and each evening before sleeping, give thanks for the good things the Creator has given you and for the opportunity to grow a little each day.

2. Show respect to the tiniest child or the oldest elder. It is a basic law of life.

3. Treat the Earth and all of her aspects as your mother. Show respect for the mineral world, the plant world, and the animal world. Do nothing to pollute the air or soil.

4. Be truthful at all times.

5. Always treat your guests with honor and consideration. Give your best food, your best blankets, the best part of your house, and your best service to your guests.

6. The hurt of one is the hurt of all; the honor of one is the honor of all.

7. Listen with courtesy to what others say, even if you feel what they are saying is worthless.

8. All the races and tribes in the world are like the different colored flowers of one meadow. All are beautiful. As children of the Creator, they must all be respected.

9. To serve others, to be of some use to family, community, nation or the world is one of the main purposes for which human beings have been created.

10. Listen to and follow the guidelines given to your heart. Guidance comes in many forms: in prayer, in dreams, in times of quiet aloneness, and in the words and deeds of wise elders and friends."

Our evenings are filled with music and dancers. My favorite evening is our last one, combining the talents of all the performers in an extraordinary concert. We are treated to Siberian throat singing; African story songs and drumming; Native American flutes and guitars; and graceful Aztec dancers in their magnificent feathered costumes. The evening culminates in a jam session that brings all of us to our feet in a joyous celebration of life.

On the last morning of the conference, the youth address the gathering. They are on fire with plans and solutions…excited to be the generation to carry on the traditions of the past, while moving ahead into the future. They offer us their most prized possessions - their youth and enthusiasm - to continue our aspirations and our work.

As we all prepare to return home, to Turtle Island, to Africa, New Zealand, Canada, Central America, and all the other corners of the globe, we carry with us the vision statement of the conference, *United in the spirit of love and respect, we heal Mother Earth and each other.*

My family spent many years, trying to trace our Cherokee lineage. We located my great-grandmother's name on the Cherokee rolls but it was difficult to get personal information about her from family members. I would look at her photograph and wish I knew her story. I was always proud of that native connection, but there's a difference between a legal connection on a piece of paper and a soul connection. I found my soul connection at this gathering of extraordinary people. I have a plaque at home that says,

Being Indian is not just what's in your blood, but what's in your heart.

After the conference, I became a member of the Appalachian American Indians of West Virginia, a tribe made up of descendants of several tribes who settled in the mountains of West Virginia, like my great-grandmother. We all share that desire to know more about our ancestors and to carry on their traditions. I try every day to honor that Algonquin grandfather's code of ethics.

In the years following that remarkable gathering, our country's environmental awareness and protection progressed, slowly. Now, I am seeing it drastically regress. I lament the current destruction to sacred land from timbering, pipelines and fracking.

I am also saddened by the deep religious and racial divisions in our country. I find myself wishing to go back to the days of that conference when old enemies united in a spirit of love and respect for Mother Earth and one another. I left the conference with hope and a strong desire to see and touch the heart of America. In the stories that follow, you will see that heart, still beating proudly and strongly in the small towns and cities of our land.

The *Belonging to Mother Earth* conference, held in Virginia Beach October 4-10, 1998, drew indigenous and Native American healers and teachers from more than 50 tribes world-wide. Over 500 conferees attended the lectures, rituals, dances, and other festivities.

SNOWMOBILING
in W. Yellowstone
is not for the faint of
heart. That's me, in
front, leading the pack.
Broke my arm the 2nd
day, while shopping.
Safer on snowmobile.

BIG, BAD BUFFALO.
I yielded right of way.

A surprise around every
bend.

Chapter 3

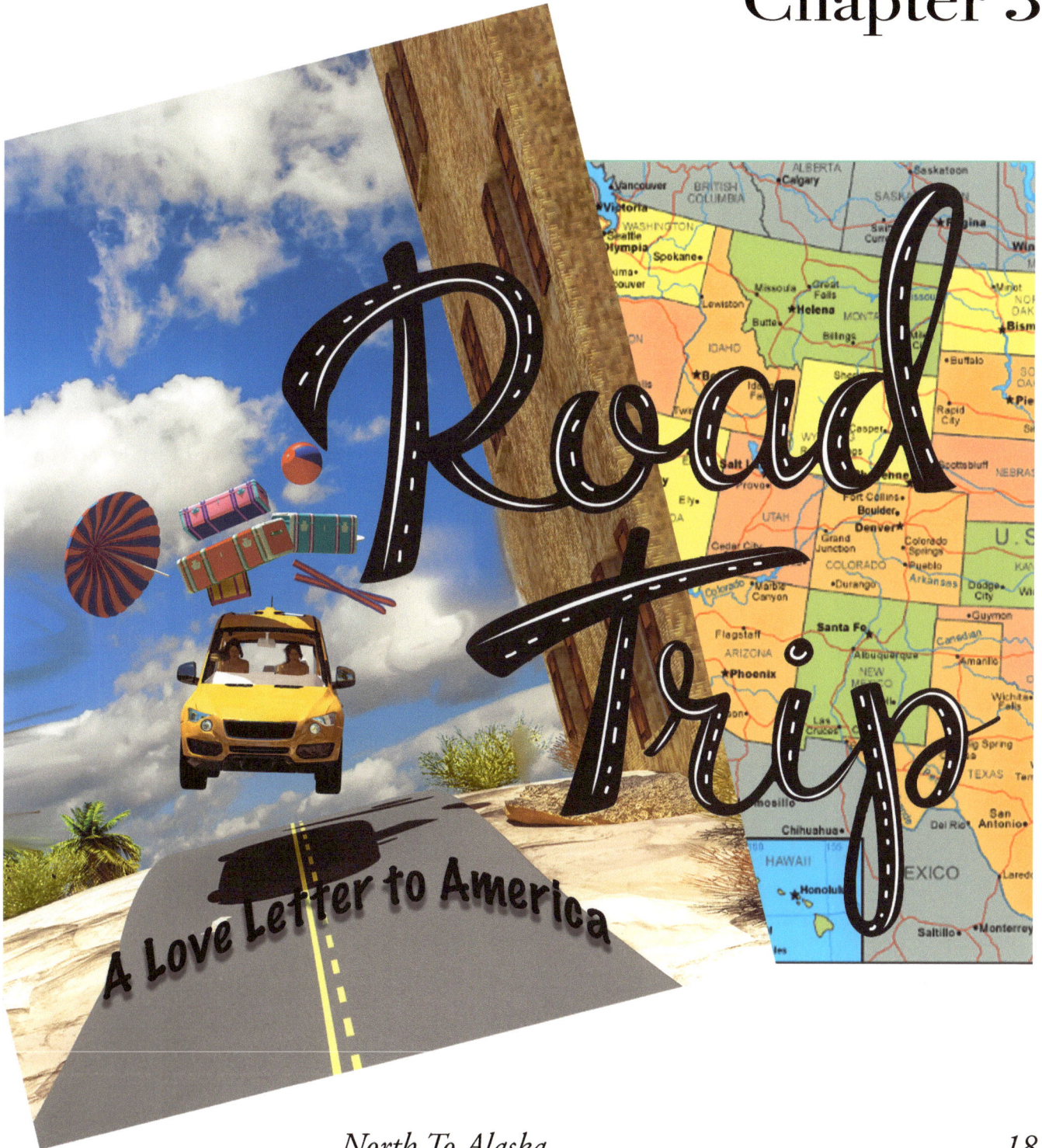

North To Alaska   18

North To Alaska

On a steaming hot day in June, Don said, "Let's go to Alaska." Any sentence with the word, "go" in it was now a good idea to me, so I said, "Yes, please, let's!" It was the beginning of a great adventure. Off we went to AAA for maps to plan the trip. We decided to enter Glacier National Park through the Montana entrance, make our way into British Columbia, up the Ice Field Parkway, over the Going to the Sun Road, through Banff and Jasper National Parks with a stop at beautiful Lake Louise.

We would drive the Al/Can (Alaska/Canada) Highway to Watson Lake, then to Whitehorse, in the Yukon Territory, and on to Haines, Alaska, ending in Skagway, Alaska, the gateway to the Klondike Gold Rush. There, we could ride the White Pass Railroad, following the route of the Stampeders at the height of the 1898 Gold Rush. We knew it was an ambitious trip but we had July and August to complete it before the snow came to the north, usually in September. We timed it pretty well - as we were driving out of Glacier, headed home, the first week in September, there were snowflakes on the windshield.

Once the plans were firm, we had to outfit our trusty vehicle, a ten-year-old Chrysler van.

The Al/Can Highway at that time was part pavement, part gravel, so we needed a screen to cover the front to protect the headlights. The van had dual fuel tanks which would be helpful in the wilderness where gas stations were few and FAR between. Our Al/Can Milepost Guide listed the gas stations, restaurants, and scenic spots along the highway. Don stocked up on oil and car parts we might need and we stowed those in a car top carrier, along with extra sleeping bags and other emergency supplies.

We took the back seats out of the van and put in a double bed mattress with a warm sleeping bag on top. It would be cold in the Yukon, even in July. Don installed some cabinets on the sides to stow our clothes and food. No fast food places on the Al/Can. We invested in a large cooler that plugged into the cigarette lighter while we were driving and would then stay cold all night. When we could, we would buy ice. We stocked lots of peanut butter and jelly, cheese, crackers, canned foods, and power bars. We were prepared with everything we could think of, including a gun, in case we had to fend off bears in the wilderness. Of course, I knew, realistically, if it came down to me, a gun and a bear, the bear would be more likely to shoot me, than vice versa. Don, on the other hand, could hold his own. Here are some of the highlights of our adventure.

Glacier National Park

It is a 2-million-acre pristine wilderness. We hiked through meadows of wild flowers, watched wild goats leap over the rocky cliffs above us, and dipped our toes (very briefly) into icy waterfalls. Even in July, there was snow on the mountain tops.

When I use the word, pristine, I mean PRISTINE. No litter along the roads, no cigarette butts in the parks, nothing. The rivers and lakes were crystal clear. We were

amazed and impressed. We could learn a lot from British Columbia.

At every stop, the views were majestic and the variety of wildflowers never-ending. We bought a book to try and identify some of them but gave up after a while and just enjoyed them. Don enjoyed them several rolls of film worth. These are just a few of the flowers we saw on our hike in Logan's Pass, Glacier Nat. Pk., B.C.

Banff National Park

Banff is huge - 2,564 sq. miles of mountains, valleys, glaciers, lakes and wild rivers. It is in Alberta, Canada, bordering Kootenay Nat. Pk., British Columbia, along the Continental Divide. Water from the Banff side of the Rocky Mountains flows to the Atlantic Ocean. Water from the Kootenay side flows to the Pacific. Kind of hard to fathom, but true.

19

Lake Louise

Located in Banff National Park, it is one of our all-time favorite gorgeous places. We braved the world of the rich and famous to have lunch in the hotel, Chateau Lake Louise. We weren't sure they'd let us dine there in our shorts and t-shirts but they did. When we paid the bill, we realized we could have bought a trunk-load of peanut butter and jelly for the cost of that meal. But we also decided it was worth it for the view alone. We dubbed it, *something for the soul.*

Athabasca Glacier And Columbia Icefield, Jasper National Park, Alberta, Canada

We actually saw the effects of global warming here at the glacier. It is retreating at an alarming pace due to accelerating use of fossil fuels, destruction of forests and release of industrial gases. Water, melting here from ice that fell as snow before the industrial revolution, is the purest natural water known. More recent snowfall carries Man's airborne pollutants. We felt fortunate to be able to see this natural wonder that is rapidly disappearing. The water from the glacier carries rock sediment into the rivers and gives them a white, milky appearance. The Columbia Icefield is still the largest body of ice in the Rocky Mountains. At its greatest depth, it is 1,200 ft.

Jasper National Park

4,200 square miles of rugged mountains, lakes and alpine valleys in the Canadian Rockies. The Icefield Parkway connects it to Banff. Fur traders settled the area in 1811, one hundred years before the railroad brought civilization. Athabasca Falls is a highlight of the park. As we hiked the trail to the top, I was surprised to see lots of tree trunks and debris that had washed down the mountain into the falls. The falls are formed from the melting water of the glacier so the water is milky white from the rock sediment. We spent several days in Jasper, did some great hikes. We also rode the cable car to the top of Whistler Mountain, which is 7,500 ft. at the top. From there, you can see the Columbia Icefields and Mt. Robson, the highest peak in the Canadian Rockies. High places are not always my friends. I held my breath most of the way up but the spectacular view was worth a little terror. There's a restaurant on top so we had lunch and heard the story about how the mountain got its name. Seems there are whistling marmots who live on the mountain, so, therefore...Really? Whistling rodents? Who knew?

Emergency Landing

The Al/Can Highway meanders through areas that look a lot like Kansas, except wheat fields instead of corn. In the flatlands, there are signs saying, *Highway Serves as Emergency Airstrip*. We read the signs, but never expected to encounter that situation.

BUT, as we came down over a hill, we were forced to screech to a halt. A small plane had landed in the middle of the narrow, two-lane road. We learned the plane had lost its fuel and the pilot had been forced to make an emergency landing.

He was young and in a state of shock. Don was a pilot and knew a lot about airplane engines from years of working on his own planes. He was able to find and repair the gas leak. The pilot radioed for help to refill the tank. As the Mounties arrived, we waved goodbye, with Don sporting a hero's grin.

The Al-Can Highway - Guts And Tractors

The story of the building of the highway is one of hardship and hope. As recently as 1940, there was no direct land route from the lower U.S. to Alaska. World War II changed all that. The highway was built out of anger after Pearl Harbor and fear that the Japanese would invade Alaska. It had to be built quickly. It would begin in

U.S. Army equipment arriving on trains at Dawson Creek, B.C.
1942

Dawson Creek and end in Fairbanks. At the peak of construction, 11,500 troops, 7,500 civilians and 11,000 pieces of equipment worked on the road, rushing to complete the job before winter halted the work. Machinery snapped, ice jams rammed pilings, streams ripped out bridges. Bogs in glacier areas swallowed trucks, tractors and sometimes, men.

Alaskan natives guided the surveyors to locate rights of way ahead of the bulldozers. The road builders faced 1,500 miles of mountains, mud, bogs, icy rivers and mosquitos. Eight and a half months later, the completed road...all 1,482 miles of it... was opened on November 20, 1942. The early roughness of the muddy road earned it the nickname, *junkyard of American cars*. Despite the obstacles, the new road promised adventure and excitement on the frontier – contacts with Indians, prospectors, Mounties, plus sled dogs, moose and grizzly bears thrown in for fun. Upgrading has continued since 1942 and $20,000,000 is spent each year to maintain what is now a mostly-paved highway through sprawling grain fields, rugged mountains, alpine forests, wildlife and spectacular wildflowers. We drove for hours, sometimes days, without meeting another vehicle or seeing another person and never knowing what was around the next bend. The Yukon still gives you that feeling of being a modern-day pioneer.

The Mysterious Yukon

Follow your heart where dreams are free,
where eagles dare to fly.
Treasure is where you find it.
Lights dance across northern skies.
There's a Spirit in these northern lands.
It rings out clear and true.
It calls you to follow the open road,
to the Trail of 42.

Watson Lake, Yukon

This community was born in 1942 as a staging area for the Alaska Highway construction. It grew from a collection of army tents into a bustling town. Today, it's famous for its signpost forest. We brought along a *Virginia is for Lovers* license plate to add to the collection. The tradition started when a homesick G.I., working on the highway, nailed up a sign, pointing the way home. Now there are more than 10,000 signs. We made a new friend while having lunch in Watson Lake (we were sick of peanut butter). He was a Japanese college student, hoping to ride his bike all the way to the Arctic Circle before the snows came. We always wondered if he made it. We bought his lunch, helped him restock his bike bags, and sent him on his way. Pioneers come in all sizes and nationalities.

The Going To The Sun Road

It is notorious for breath-taking views and *cars going over the side* accidents. There are no guard rails. Some stretches have flat rock barriers; some do not. The road was apparently designed by a vertigo-inclined engineer with a fear of heights who was trying to get over both at the same time. The road winds up the side of the cliffs in one of the most rugged areas of the Rockies. Our van is tall and didn't exactly hug the road, which made it even scarier. Add to that, Don's inclination to try and look over the edge while driving and well, you get the picture. If I ever travel that road again, it will be with a paper bag over my head. Just tell me when it's over!

Going To The Sun Road

Winding in and winding out,
fills my mind with serious doubt
as to whether the *lout* who planned this route,
was going to hell or coming out.

Whitehorse

The Yukon capital was a sleepy little village until the highway came through and changed all that. It now has a population of over 20,000 but it has kept its pioneer spirit. Log cabins share the streets with modern office buildings. We had a good time there. We toured the Klondike, which is a pristine, restored paddlewheel boat. I have wanted to take a paddlewheel cruise ever since. We had dinner in the Klondike Saloon and saw a funny musical revue. It's a *Yukon Postcard* of a town with little gardens everywhere, complete with benches where we could sit and enjoy the flowers. We wanted to stay longer but ALASKA was calling, FINALLY, just around a few more bends in the road.

Haines, Alaska

We drove onto the ferry to Haines on a foggy morning and the rain followed us all the way to our destination. We'd been warned about the Alaskan rain so were prepared with raincoats. The ferry traveled close to the shore so we could watch for wildlife and were rewarded with sightings of brown bears and moose. Haines is a gathering place for eagles. As many as 3,500 come to the Chilkat River in the fall to feast on late-returning salmon. Haines is a stronghold of Indian culture and a mecca for artists. We attended a potlatch and dined on the best salmon I've ever tasted, sweet and pink, grilled over red cedar chips and served on red cedar slabs. We were treated to a program by the world-famous Chilkat Dancers and admired, up close, the intricate workmanship of the hand-made blankets. Amazing totems dotted the landscape and we spent a morning watching the craftsmen and women carving these masterpieces in wood. We kept trying to figure out how we could bring one home in the van.

CHILKAT DANCERS

Alaska, The Great Land

The Aleuts called it Alyeska, which means, The Great Land. It is one thing to read about Alaska's majestic scale and quite another to experience it. It is a land of rain forests, of timeless rituals. When nature sings her ancient songs, birds wing their way north, and salmon and whales begin an annual odyssey encompassing thousands of miles. This is a land of mountain spires, mighty rivers and whispering breezes.

The Sublime To The Ridiculous

The earliest peoples arrived when the land was still very young. Nomadic tribes crossed from Siberia to North America on a land bridge, long since vanished, which connected the two continents. They became the ancestors of those who have settled in the Aleutian Islands, the Far North, Southeast Alaska, as well as other American Indian nations in the Lower 48. These early Alaskans adapted well to the harsh environment and created a spiritual world rich in tradition and culture.

They lived peaceful lives until Russian sailors sighted the mainland in 1741 and staked a claim. They were soon followed by British, Spanish and American adventurers. When their fur trade declined, the Russians lost interest in this unexplored land. U. S. Secretary of State, William Seward, was able to purchase it from them in 1867 for $7,200,000. He was ridiculed for his decision and not much attention was paid to the distant land until 1880, when Joe Juneau and Richard Harris stumbled into a gold-laden creek in Southeast Alaska.

Their find attracted a few prospectors, but it wasn't until 1897 that the big Gold Rush began, bringing 100,000 fortune hunters to the Klondike gold fields. Prospectors braved raging storms and treacherous, rocky slopes as they struggled to cross the legendary Chilkoot Pass to the rivers that would take them to the gold fields. Most of the men who survived the journey, went home broke and disappointed.

Skagway, Alaska – Gold Rush Town

When you enter Skagway, you step through time, to a place where the past feels real and very present; where cries of *Gold in the Yukon,* still seem to echo from steep canyon walls; and the sounds of barroom pianos ring out in the night. Skagway saw tens of thousands of prospectors in 1898. They got off steamships to head overland to the gold fields by way of the White Pass Trail or the Chilkoot Trail. But before the lonely men could leave town, they faced the temptations of eighty saloons, the lure of painted ladies and the quick fingers of gamblers. Skagway is *history come to life* in buildings dating to the Gold Rush. We could have spent a month in this charming town. There was so much to see and do, including panning for gold. We did find specks of gold, but, alas, no nuggets.

White Pass Railroad

It is called the *railway built of gold*. It was constructed at the height of the 1898 Klondike Gold Rush. It leaves from Skagway and follows the route of the Stampeders. It is considered one of the world's greatest engineering feats. We understood why as we traveled through tunnels and around curves that took our breath away if we dared to look down the sheer cliffs. All along the route you can see rusty gear and debris abandoned by the miners as they fought their way up the trail. We rode in the open-air part of the observation car so Don could take photos. He would have climbed on top if he could!

Headed Home, Via The Cassiar Highway

Whenever we travel, we always want to see as many new places as possible, so we decided to take a different route south than the Al-Can Highway which brought us north. We were warned that the Cassiar was a favorite truckers' route, busier than the Alaska/Canada Highway. We decided to try it anyway and I'm so glad we did. On our second day back on the road, we were amazed to discover a small church and a huge field of totems—all sizes, all kinds.

Totem poles are the carved wooden posts for which the native people of the region, especially the Haida, are famous. Originally, totem poles were used as supports for houses. Later, they became free-standing ornamentation. Common carvings on a totem pole are the raven, owl, beaver, eagle and supernatural creatures.

These totems were very old and weathered and some had actually fallen down and were lying on the ground, half covered in weeds. Nobody was around, no houses nearby, just the little empty church. We decided it was a graveyard of totems. I felt peaceful, connected to the ancestors, walking among them and was sorry when we had to move on down the road. It was my favorite experience of the trip. Happiness is my very own field of totems.

Civilization—Must We????

So much to ooh and aah over on the trip south - more glaciers, majestic mountains, rolling rivers and peaceful lakes. AND THEN--wouldn't you know--road work! We knew blaring horns and fast food restaurants were just around the bend.

True confession…we almost turned around and went back. There's something about the wilderness that puts things in perspective and soothes the soul. We hoped to carry that feeling with us as we returned to *real life*.

Sharon Canfield Dorsey

Zion National Park, Utah,
is breath-taking in winter.

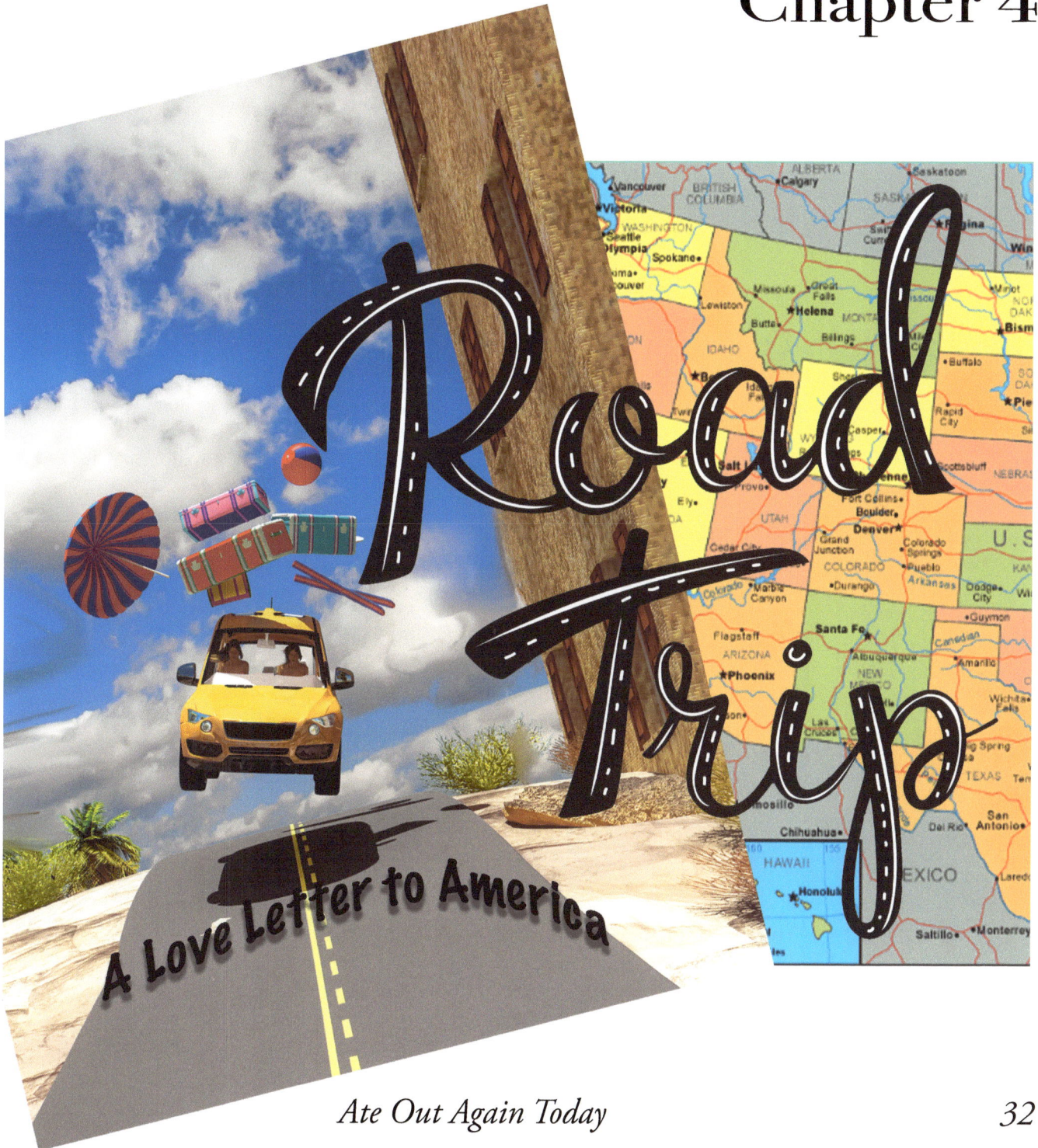

Chapter 4

Road Trip

A Love Letter to America

Ate Out Again Today

I once saw a postcard in a gift shop with a picture of a pioneer woman in a sunbonnet, bending over a campfire in front of a Conestoga wagon. The caption was, *Ate out again today.* I can relate to that woman. I recently spent two months eating out of a 22 ft. tin can on wheels, driven by a modern-day Lewis/Clark.

How Hot Was It?

Our relationship had already survived one near disastrous cross-country tent camping trip. After a few nights of sleeping out in the Southwest's 102-degree temperatures, I rebelled and demanded air conditioning and a shower without lizards. Don not only complied, he did so in a big way, using his Retired Air Force Colonel status to get us accommodations in the VIP quarters of a nearby military base. That did it! The tent didn't leave the trunk again on that trip. When I unpacked the car after we returned home, I made sure the tent found its way to the highest shelf in the garage, never to be seen again.

Alaska in a Van

On the Alaska wilderness trip, we had moved up the travel ladder a little, outfitting our van with a comfortable mattress, a camp stove, and a portable toilet. But after that two months on the road, I DREAMED of a real bathroom with a shower. When we returned, the tent on the top shelf in the garage was joined by the portable toilet, along with the shovel we'd used to bury its contents.

A Tin Can on Wheels

We began going to RV shows but everything was too big or too grand for our gypsy travel style. We agreed we wanted something small enough to drive the back roads and camp in wilderness areas. We also agreed RVs are all a little like tin cans on wheels, but, we reminded ourselves, they had real stoves and bathrooms. We settled on a 22 ft. Itaska – filled the cabinets with dishes and food, the closet with jeans and t-shirts and stashed our shampoos and toothbrushes in the bathroom. We felt luxurious! Before I could learn the words to *Get Your Kicks on Route 66,* we were on the road again, traveling in style.

I had never seen Don so excited. I had gotten a little caught up in the hype myself. Our home-away-from-home was cozy, with its tiny kitchen and minuscule bathroom. It was like playing house--romantic and quaint--I thought. I had a lot to learn.

The first lesson was preparing our bed. Before leaving home, we practiced creating a bed from the table top and cushions. That part was easy. Getting around the table, now the bed, was not so easy, resulting in bruised knees and shins.

We eventually worked out a system for going to bed and getting up. We undressed first, took turns in the bathroom, and then made the bed. The only glitch came when someone sleeping in the back needed to *go* in the middle of the night. There *was* a bright side to the inconvenience. There could be no late-night snacking, because we couldn't open the refrigerator door. I was sure I would be svelte by the time we returned home.

I had planned a special dinner for our first night on the road. We checked into the RV park and I sent Don out to have manly discussions with the other guys who had also been kicked out. I set the table carefully, lit candles and turned my attention to the food. This was fun!

I chopped the veggies for our favorite stir fry on my miniature cutting board and turned on the gas stove. Nothing happened. I tried again. Nothing. I yelled out the door, "Honey, would you turn on the gas?" I got that *deer in the headlights* look. He had forgotten to fill the propane tank. I arranged the veggies artistically on the brand-new plates and Don, who hates salad, declared it was the best dinner he'd ever eaten.

The ants came onboard sometime during our second night on the road and joined us for breakfast. Despite our best efforts to evict them, they remained steadfast halfway across the country, surfacing for dinner and disappearing when it was gone. On the third day, they were joined by big, grey moths who emerged from the overhead vents. We hoped the moths would dine on the ants but apparently, they had found something tastier in the vents for they also would disappear during the day, only to fly out again when we turned on the ceiling fan in the evening.

We kept looking back as we passed through field after field of Kansas corn and giant sunflowers to be sure a swarm of hungry locusts wasn't trailing behind. Kansas actually turned out to be our happy place. The ants and moths disembarked somewhere, probably from boredom during the endless drive across the Sunflower State, never to be seen again.

Every night, Don would study his maps and plan our next day's adventures. But sometimes the best adventures were un-planned. We spent a lot of time on the back roads, sometimes lost, or as Mr. Lewis/Clark described it, "in unexpected surroundings."

On a leisurely drive down the Oregon coast, we found ourselves in "unexpected surroundings," bumping along a rocky road that narrowed to one lane, with thick bushes and trees on both sides of the road. There was nothing to do but follow it to its end. Just when we thought we were going to have to hike out for help, the road emerged from the trees and in the clearing was a white sand beach, wiped clean of every footprint. We spread our blanket on the sand, ate our peanut butter sandwiches and watched the sinking sun finger-paint the sky in hues of palest pink to flaming orange. We sat in the sand, holding hands, till the last trace of rose faded from the horizon. The seals barked goodnight as we climbed the hill to our home on wheels.

We had no time schedule as we wandered around the country. We stopped when we saw something interesting, slept when we were tired, and moved on when we felt like it. But I insisted on being in Salt Lake City, Utah, for the 4th of July. Nobody does that family holiday better than our Mormon friends.

There is a wonderful sameness about 4th of July parades.

- The high school bands, red-faced in 100-degree heat, but high-stepping, with faithful moms running along the sidelines, spritzing the kids with water and looking as if they need someone to spritz them.

- The awkward, little girl dance troupes, with gangly legs and sparkly costumes, brandishing batons and toothless grins that turn parents and grandparents into lumps of loving goo.

- Acres of Boy and Girl Scouts, in uniforms plastered with patches and medals.

- Politicians, flashing winning smiles, aimed at gaining votes in the next election.

- Antique cars, driven by antique grandmas and grandpas, waving and throwing candy to the kids on the sidelines.

- Papier-mâché floats, transporting beauty queens in glittering crowns and fairytale gowns.

Two things were extra special in this parade.

- A van filled with Special Olympics athletes that got more applause than the politicians.

- Dozens of tattooed Harley dudes and chicks on bikes, escorting a float filled with laughing kids, identified by a huge sign, "Bikers against child abuse."

My favorite part of the parade was last -- everyone in the crowd standing, hats off and hands over hearts, as Old Glory passed by, escorted proudly by the high school drill team and followed by the Veterans of Foreign Wars, in faded uniforms and polished boots.

Lessons I Learned On My Summer Vacation

Vacations used to leave me with memories of beaches or mountains and shoe boxes full of faded snapshots. This 12,000-mile adventure across America from Atlantic to Pacific, left Don and me with vivid mental snapshots of the heart of our land. In my search for a definition of who we have become, we Americans, I found the good, the bad and the ugly. But mostly, I found our heartbeat strong and full of pride. I also learned some unexpected lessons.

Patriotism Is Alive!

I learned the Pennsylvania Dutch and Amish farm families around Lancaster Co., PA, know how to celebrate Independence Day. Small flags wave in neat rows across their lawns. Red, white and blue bunting decorates their porches and advertises their patriotism. They gather together for ice cream socials and picnics, and their children know the true meaning of this most important holiday. Our Founding Fathers would be proud.

Corn, Corn, Everywhere...

The cornfields of Kansas look very much like those of Iowa and Nebraska. But South Dakota rewards the weary traveler with shining fields of golden sunflowers, stretching for miles into the horizon.

RV Parks And Art Galleries

RV parks are as varied as the vehicles parked there. Our overnight homes ranged from lush parks to concrete pads. My favorite was a small, quiet campground in Grants Pass, Oregon. It was an outdoor art gallery, with whimsical sculptures and wood carvings, all crafted and shared with much pride by the owner.

If You Don't Like The Weather, Just Wait

I learned to appreciate 55 degrees in Washington and Oregon after 105 degrees in Iowa and Nebraska. I even learned to like cold showers in unheated bathhouses inhabited by tiny lizards. Well, almost.

Goodness And Honesty Still Exist

There are nice people in Lewiston, Montana, who not only repaired our ailing transmission at a fair price, but loaned us their personal car, packed us a picnic lunch, and sent us off with a map to explore their little town while we were waiting for the repairs to be finished. News travels fast in a small town and every place we went, we were treated as special guests.

Yes, There Really Is A Corn Palace

In Mitchell, S. D., there is a magnificent palace covered in corn kernels and multi-hued corn husks. It is refurbished every year with a new design. The townspeople work for weeks to create this remarkable building. It is an expression of pride in their farming community.

All Men Are Created Equal -- Not Always

Sadly, many Native Americans on the Sioux, Crow and Navaho reservations still exist in squalor and poverty.

Rusting car bodies litter the parched yards of small, square-box houses in need of paint. Faded laundry bakes on sagging lines in the boiling sun. Jobs are difficult to find and young people leave school too soon. Drug and alcohol addiction are commonplace.

A lucky few escape to college. Some return to the reservation to help the hopeless. Such is the case of a beautiful Lakota Sioux woman in Chamberlain, South Dakota. She grew up in a Catholic boarding school for orphans because her parents had too many children. She graduated, went on to college and is now back home. We met her in the small art gallery she has opened to help market the crafts of her people. She also works as a housemother in the orphanage where she grew up. She is teaching the Sioux children to have pride in their heritage and she is making a difference in many small lives.

Family Reunions Are All The Same

Whether they are held in a city park or on an Indian reservation, family reunions are a lot alike. Our new Lakota friend invited us to attend a Pow Wow, which is a family reunion, but with drums and dancers. We were greeted by young teens on ponies, racing over the gently sloping grasslands. As we wandered around, we saw older teens in jeans with spiked hair, looking bored and above it all. Giggling little girls behaved like giggling little girls everywhere. Grandmothers in long, brightly-colored dresses and braids gossiped while their men gathered in small circles, smoking, not talking much. Barefoot babies slept on patchwork quilts on the grass, guarded by proud mothers. The haunting cry of a flute filtered through the trees, carried on the wind. The unrelenting beat of the drums echoed across the plains as these First People of our land, proclaimed their ancestral pride with their dances and their regalia of deerskin and feathers.

The Impossible Takes A Little Longer

My visit to Crazy Horse Mountain in South Dakota taught me that the human spirit is indomitable. Some people refuse to give up their dreams, despite seemingly insurmountable obstacles. Case in point -- Korczak Ziolkowski, a Polish sculptor. He spent 50 years carving a gigantic figure of Chief Crazy Horse into the granite of the Black Hills as a tribute to the native people. He died in 1982 with only the head of the carving completed. But his wife, children and grandchildren are carrying on the dream. The completed figure of the Sioux chief, seated on his horse, arm outstretched, will be 563 feet tall, larger than the presidential figures on Mt. Rushmore.

Pride In Stone

At Mt. Rushmore, I discovered I can still be awe-struck. The first sight of the mountain makes your heart jump in surprise. As you approach the park by vehicle, it is suddenly there—so visible, so accessible and so grand. We've all seen photos but none do justice to this masterpiece. When I visited the crude studio of the creator, Gutson Borglum, looked at the original models, then out the window at the real thing, I was humbled at the artist's genius and vision. He felt such pride in being an American, that he wanted to give something back. He gave us a treasure.

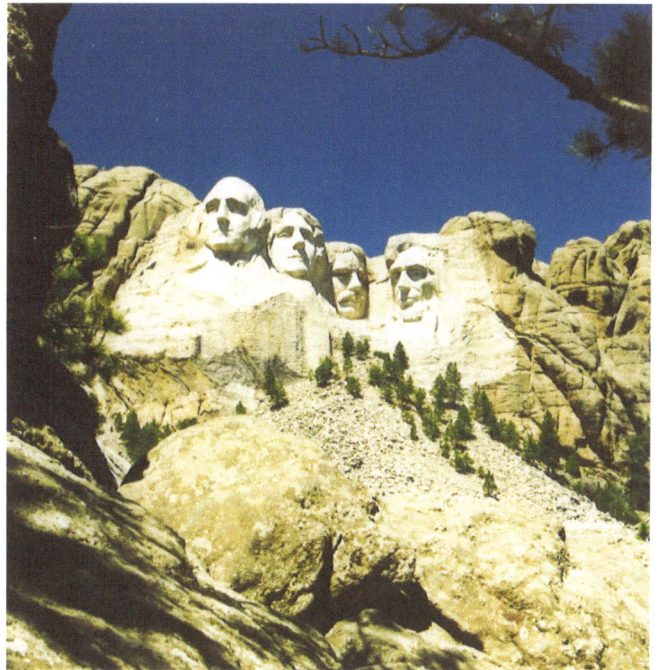

Lively Ghost Towns

As we continued through Wyoming, I discovered that sagebrush can be as boring as Kansas cornfields. But here, the names of the cities kept my imagination awake and working overtime —Sundance, Buffalo, Billings and Bighorn evoked images of Indian battles and Gold Rush towns. My mind's eye filled the sagebrush with boisterous life.

Independence Begins Early

In Wyoming, there is a massive basalt mountain, called Devil's Tower, that rises 867 feet above its base, which is 1,000 feet in diameter.

Huge boulders litter the hillside leading up to the tower. They present a tricky challenge for climbers. I gave up after a short distance and climbed onto a big rock to watch. Sharing my perch was a Native American family, attentively watching three young teenagers scramble to the base, pose for the standard triumphant photo and then carefully make their way down. The three were agile and made the trip up and back very quickly. But the family continued to watch two other figures, descending slowly. I learned it was a mother and five-year-old daughter. I watched with them as the mother took one small step at a time and instructed the little girl to follow in her footsteps. The husband/father watched nervously as the pair neared the bottom. He ran over to meet them, reaching out to lift the beaming child over the last big boulder. The mother stopped him and I heard her say, "No, let her find her way. She must feel pride in herself."

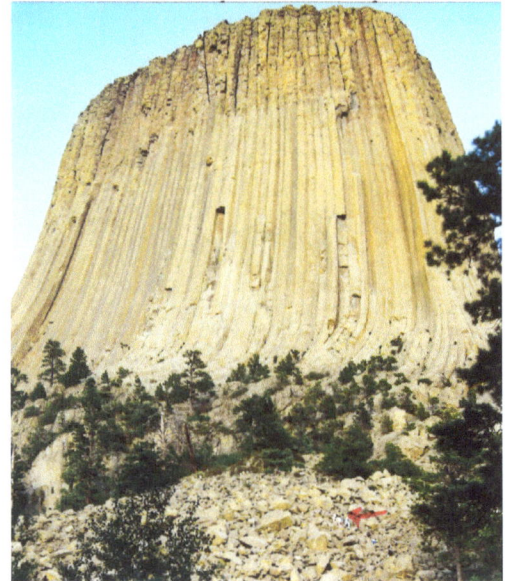

What If???

In Montana, I was surprised to learn that eleven Indian tribes live on reservations in this state...the Crow, Blackfeet, Flathead, Northern Cheyenne, Assiniboine, Sioux, Gros Ventre, Chippewa, Cree, Salish, and Kootenai. One has to wonder how different our crowded, polluted land would be today if these eco-conscious people had been allowed to remain on their own lands, caring for them and about them.

From Shocking To Historic

The tiny town of Wallace, Idaho illustrates how time can put an entirely different perspective on an event, changing the scandalous into the quaint. This small silver mining town, population 1,010, is listed in its entirety in the Historical Register. The original buildings now house museums.

The most interesting is the Bordello Museum, telling the story, without apology, of the ladies of the evening. Their patrons often left in a hurry, leaving behind everything from their long johns to bags of groceries. The museum displays many of these fascinating objects.

At the end of the tour, we were informed that the brothel began operation in 1895 and closed in 1989. Yes, that's right, 1989.

Priceless Trivia

Kansas and Missouri filled my journal with trivia jewels.

- The Barbed Wire Museum in LaCrosse, Kansas, features more than 500 different types of the prickly stuff. Who knew??

- Only Rome, Italy has more fountains than Kansas City, Missouri. It also claims the dubious honor of having built America's first shopping center.

- It was once illegal to serve ice cream on cherry pie in Kansas. Nobody seemed to know why.

- If you're having a less than wonderful family vacation and want to lose the kids for a while, the corn maze in Buhler, Kansas is the place to go. They do, however, insist that you collect them before dark.

Is This Really Progress?

While spending several sun-filled days cruising the blue-green waters of Lake Powell in Utah, I reconfirmed my conviction that progress is not always best. High on a sheer, rocky cliff in the middle of the lake is one of the few remaining Anasasi ruins in the area. I grieved for all the beauty and history lost when the other ruins were flooded by the Glen Canyon Dam. True, it is a beautiful recreation area, enjoyed by boaters, but in the process, we have deliberately destroyed the story of a civilization.

The Raven's Lament

They vanished hundreds of years ago,
the ancient ones, the gatherers.
They told stories of their lives
on cave walls and picture rocks.
They left pottery and tools in their granaries
and rocky hillside houses.
But we flooded their homes
and forever erased their history.
Now we drive powerboats through the waters
covering their hunting grounds,
and only the circling ravens know their secrets,
proclaiming their stories in their haunting laments.

A Cheese Lovers Delight...

In Tillamook, Oregon, I watched my favorite food being made at the largest cheese factory in the state. Unfortunately, I learned that watching those delicious cheeses being made doesn't alter the "hand to waist" calorie progression.

Paradise Found

On the Oregon coast, I delighted in deserted beaches, reminding me of something important I'd forgotten in my busy life at home. Solitude is good for the soul. Forever etched in my memory is a sunset, so breathtakingly beautiful, I thought, "If I were to die here, in this place, in this perfect moment, it would be OK." Everyone should have a moment like that.

Hooray For Mysteries

In the Oregon Vortex, in Gold Hill, Oregon, I found that even the most astute scientific minds can't explain everything. In the "House of Mystery," balls roll uphill, short people appear taller and vice-versa. Engineers have conducted over 14,000 experiments and can only explain the phenomenon as a "whirlpool of invisible energy."

Why Are We Cutting Old Growth Trees?

The towering redwoods in Northern California taught me a valuable lesson in humility. How insignificant our life span, compared to the 2000+ life span of the great trees. What stories they could tell and how sad so few remain. The mountains above the coast have been devastated by loggers. That's a lesson I wish I hadn't learned.

It's a Small World

In a little community, just inside the California state line, I was reminded that sometimes things happen the way they are intended. We passed a tiny Native American craft shop, half hidden in the middle of a lily field, and quickly, did one of our now-accomplished U-turns. Inside, I found treasure. During the trip, I had been searching for just the right jewelry for my "mother of the bride" dress for daughter, Shannon's, Cherokee wedding, which would take place when we returned.

I described my dress and the owner of the shop, a Tolala Indian, said his wife could make the jewelry for me. A look around provided all the other things I needed for the ceremony —a wedding vase, baskets for the potlatch gifts, and wonderful hand-crafted feather boxes for the two Cherokee officiants.

When I pulled out one of my Mary Kay Cosmetics business cards to provide a mailing address for the jewelry, which would be sent later, the man smiled and said, "My wife is a Mary Kay Beauty Consultant, too." I left, knowing I had made two new friends.

Kayaking in the San Juans

In the waters surrounding Orcas Island in the San Juan Islands, off the coast of Seattle, I learned that going out kayaking for the first time can be daunting. The first lesson was getting into the strange gear. The second lesson  was how to step into the boat, wearing the gear, without tipping it over. I flunked, requiring a do-over. The third lesson was how to handle the paddle without whacking the friend who was instructing me, in the head. After all that, it was smooth gliding through the clear, blue water, UNTIL, I heard a horn in the distance and looked over my shoulder to see a three-stories-tall ferry, headed straight for us. We paddled like crazy for shore and all ended well.

Killer Whales I Met

Orcas Island is named for the gentle giants (7 ton) who reside year 'round in the waters surrounding the San Juan Islands. There are over a hundred killer whales in three pods (families) who roam miles through the islands to feed and play. Each Orca has been given a name by researchers who have been working in the area for years and has been identified as a member of a specific family. On a foggy morning, we bundled up and headed off on one of the small research boats in search of Orcas. Actually, they found us, peeping black shiny noses out of the water to rub on the sides of the boat, then swim off to perform amazing acrobatics for us. By the end of the day, we had been visited by all three pods—an incredible sight. The scientists were as amazed as we were, confessing they had never seen all three pods in one location--a once in a lifetime adventure.

Mother Nature's Beauty and Wrath

Two separate day-hikes in the Seattle, Washington area, gave me perfect examples of those two things -- the incredible beauty and quiet peace of the forests and cliffs of Mt. Ranier vs. the catastrophic aftermath of Mt. St. Helen's fury. Looking across that vast wasteland at acres of downed trees, like match sticks in the distance, brought home the reality of nature's power. I kept remembering that old line, "Don't mess with Mother Nature."

Man-Made Disaster

Olympic National Park in Washington State is a wonderland of deep green rain forests and gigantic trees. But timbering is taking a terrible toll on those forests and the aftermath washes up on the beaches at Ocean Shores, near the park. How sad to see all those skeletons of trees past.

Revenge on Litterers

As we visited our beautiful state and national parks, it became obvious that we have become a nation of slobs. Litter is everywhere, often on the ground near a trash can. One woman, who parked beside us at a visitor center and emptied her ashtray on the ground by her car, may think twice before doing it again. When she went inside, leaving her white convertible top down, we returned the contents of her ashtray to her (and beat a hasty retreat).

Many thousand miles and many adventures later, I am home, suntanned, ten pounds lighter, and rattling around in a townhouse that suddenly seems huge. Last night, I couldn't sleep, so I crept out to the RV, crawled into my table/bed and fell instantly to sleep, dreaming of 4th of July parades, orange sunsets and Conestoga wagons.

LAND OF THE FREE AND HOME OF THE BRAVE

When did we become a land of "Any City," U. S. A,
with shopping malls and parking lots where antelope once played?

And who decided we should harvest all the old growth trees,
once home to nesting birds and busy hives of buzzing bees?

And where, in writing, does it say, that progress is the best,
that here and there should be a park, and overcrowd the rest?

Who thinks that we should trash the land, the heavens and the sea?
No one speaks up, accepts the blame. It's left to you and me.

The attitude is that we aren't the keeper of our brother.
Look out for number one without concern for one another.

We share this ship, this Mother Earth, suspended high above.
We can't survive or prosper here, unless we learn to love.

Love creatures, large and small, who dwell upon this land.
Love trees, and fresh clean air, and mountains that are grand.

For what we love, we will protect and nurture till day's end.
And then, perhaps, our home, the earth, will slowly start to mend.

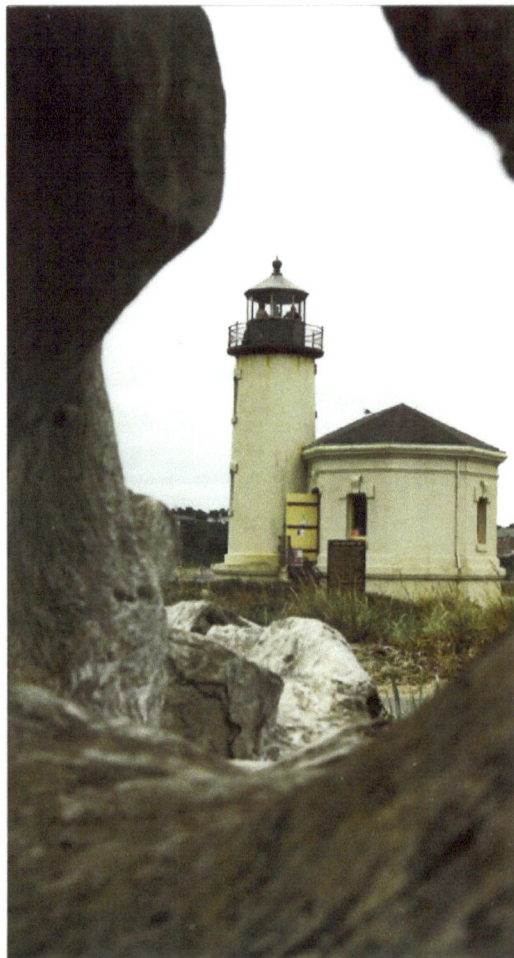

OREGON COAST has an intriguing lighthouse around every turn, deserted beaches with gorgeous sunsets, PLUS, cheese factories! WHAT'S NOT TO LOVE???

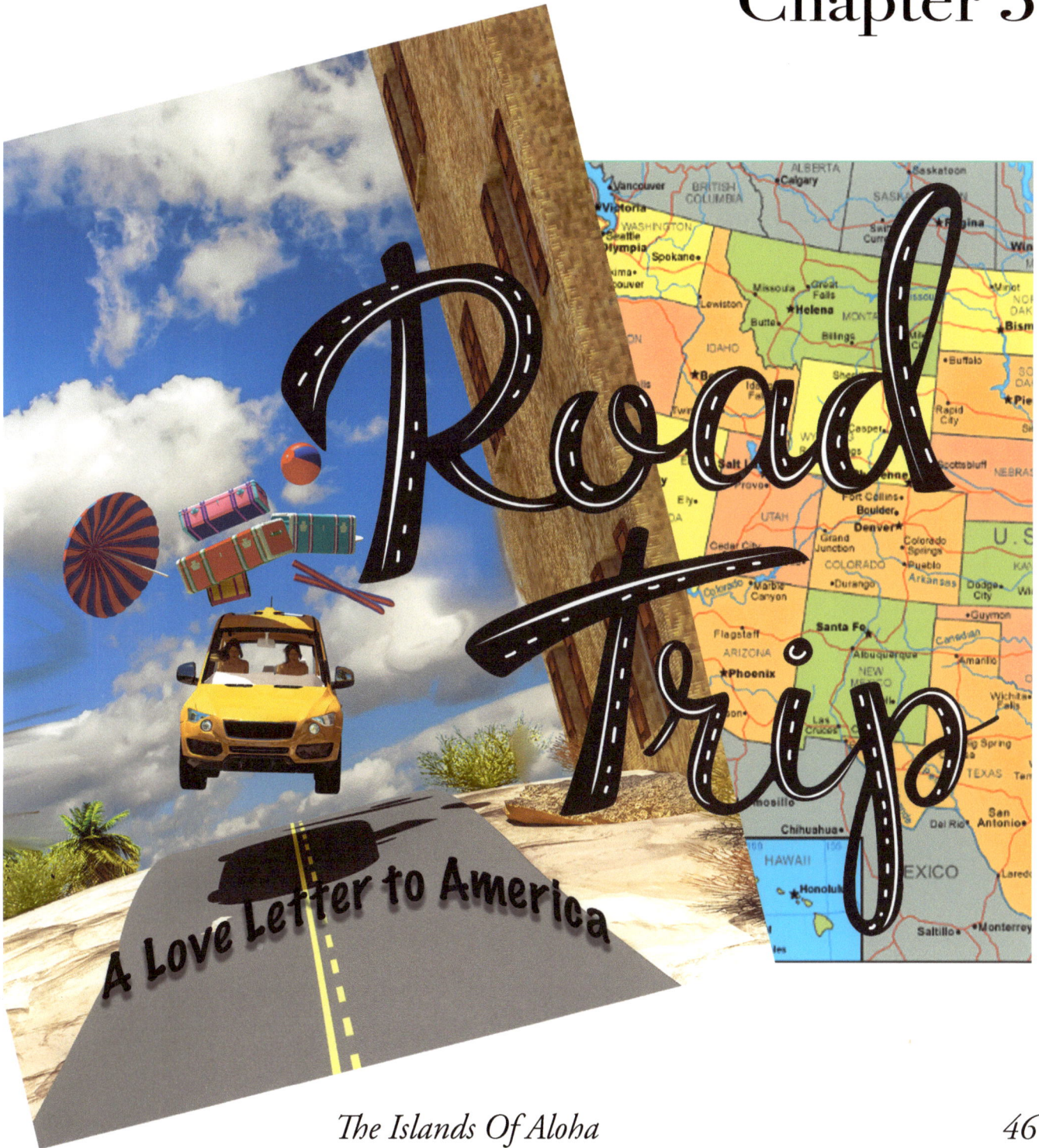

Chapter 5

Road Trip

A Love Letter to America

The Islands Of Aloha

"How would you like to celebrate your 50th birthday in Hawaii?" Don asked.

The only answer was – "YES, YES, YES! When can we leave????"

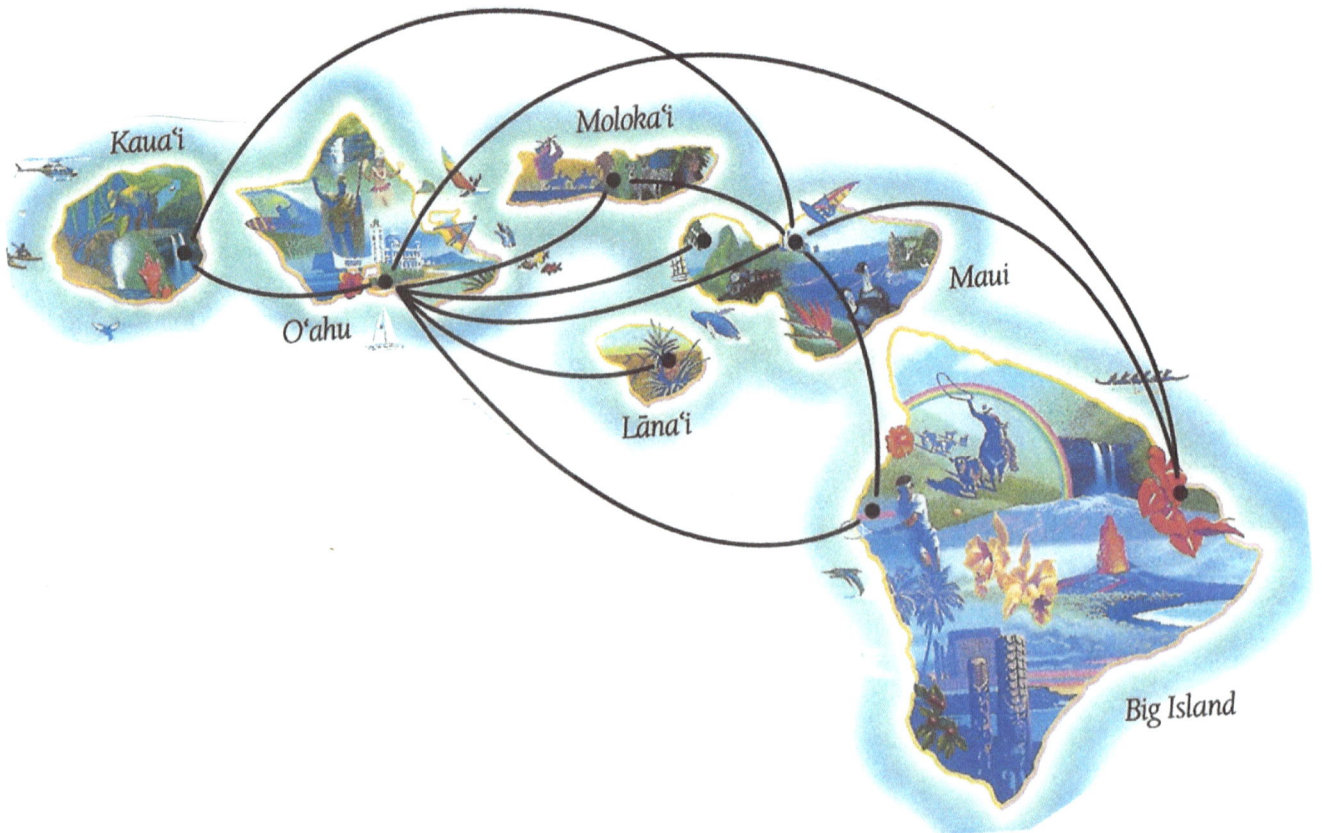

Getting to Hawaii is no picnic. We flew cross country to California, had a four hour lay-over and then flew on to Oahu, landing early in the morning of SOME day – we weren't quite sure with all the time changes, etc. I'd been too excited to sleep much and was a little bleary-eyed. But it didn't matter. It was HAWAII and I had dreamed of this day since I was a teenager. It was a perfect 80-degree day, flower-scented breeze, blue skies, and someone was placing a beautiful lei of purple orchids around my neck. I couldn't stop smiling.

That would be the pattern of the next three weeks -- perfect weather, incredible beauty, and me -- always smiling. We had planned the trip carefully -- not our usual pattern -- with our travel agent/friend, Sue, in order to see as much of the islands as we could in the time we had. We island-hopped by small planes, picked up a rental car or jeep on each island, and then went off to explore on our own. We had requested to stay in B&B's or small hotels and Sue found wonderful places for us where we met local characters who made our visit so much more interesting. When it was time to go home, I didn't want to leave. I experienced such a strong soul connection there. I've visited a lot of beautiful places but the Islands of Aloha remain my favorite.

Oahu, The Gathering Place

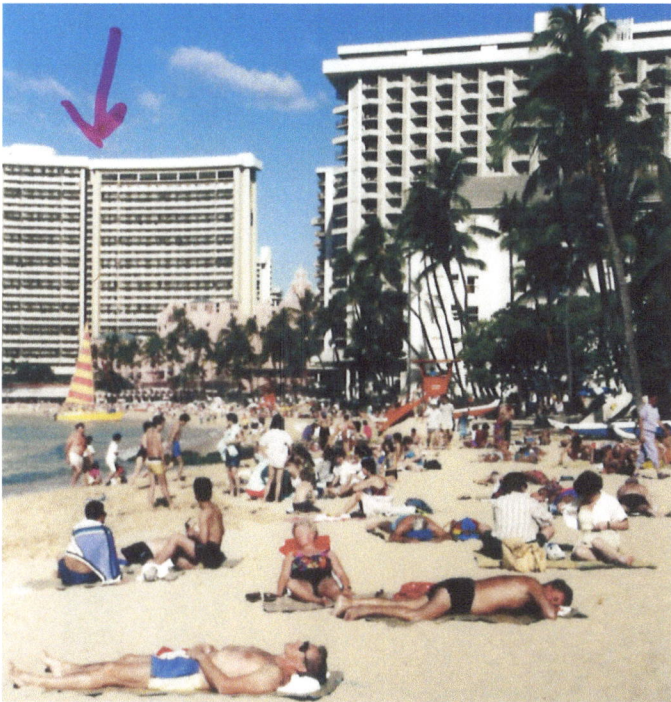

More than 4/5ths of Hawaii's population live here. Honolulu is a bustling, cosmopolitan city. Waikiki Beach is jammed with tourists. But get out of the city and you find lofty mountains, roaring surf and the quiet beauty of Waimea Falls. You also find the Polynesian Cultural Center.

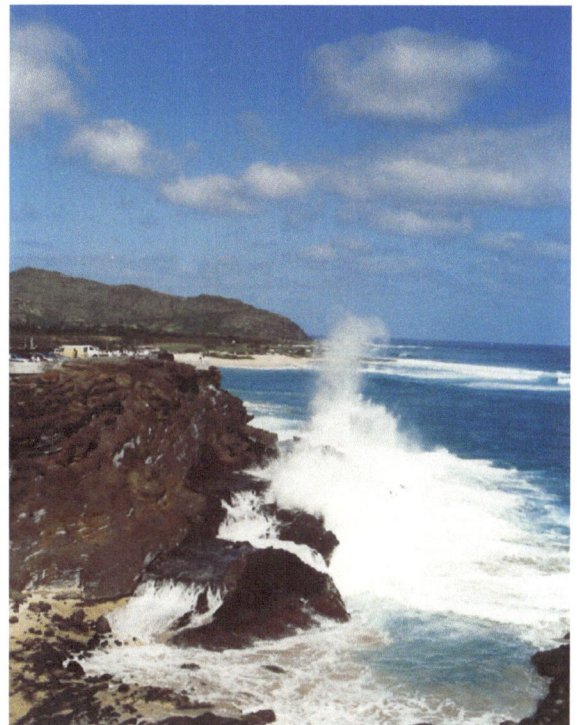

We were fortunate to be able to stay at the Hale Koa Hotel on Waikiki, a military R&R facility which accommodates active duty and retired military families at a reasonable price. Don commented that those 31 years in the Air Force had finally paid off.

The Polynesian Cultural Center encompasses 42 acres on Oahu's North Shore, where you can learn about and experience the cultures of all the islands of Polynesia -- FIJI, HAWAII, TAHITI, SAMOA, NEW ZEALAND, TONGA, MARQUESAS. The center was founded by the Mormon Church to "preserve the heritage of Polynesia," and provide educational opportunities (and employment) for students at nearby Brigham Young University. Whatever the purpose, it is an amazing experience. We spent an entire day-- pigged out (literally-- roast pig with apple in mouth) at the Luau and enjoyed the nighttime show, complete with music, dancers from all the islands, AND fire-eaters.

Kauai, The Garden Isle

Kauai is a wonderland of waterfalls, canyons and tropical rain forests.

Trivia Note… "Raiders of the Lost Ark" was filmed here. We paddled through a rainy fern grotto that could have been a movie set. We were told it is a favorite exotic wedding location. Kauai also boasts a post-volcanic canyon that is called the Grand Canyon of the Pacific. The Grand Canyon in Arizona is one of Don's favorite places, so of course, we had to drive to the summit to compare the views. I was amazed at the spectacular similarities.

Kauai is a beachcombers delight. The sea is cobalt blue and the sand feels like silk beneath your feet. No wonder Hollywood chose this island as the backdrop for "South Pacific," Elvis Presley's "Blue Hawaii," and television's "Fantasy Island." Kauai is also famous for its beautiful flowers. Of all the islands, I was looking forward to this one the most. BUT, a hurricane came through two weeks before our trip, clipping the tops off palm trees, roofs off buildings, and devastating the flowers. We had difficulty finding places to stay but still enjoyed our visit there, despite the complications. All part of the adventure.

Maui, The Valley Isle

Maui gave me the one thing that was missing on Kauai, glorious flowers, everywhere -- orchids, hibiscus, plumeria -- some flowers I recognized and lots I didn't. My flower philosophy is, "Flowers are for picking." I wanted to take all of them home with me. I did carry home a florist box full of exotic blooms.

The volcanic craters of Haleakala and the black lava beaches of Hana are in unique contrast to the white sand beaches on the other side of the island. We drove the 55-mile trip to Hana, past towering waterfalls, lava cliffs, lush rain forests, sugar cane fields, and banana trees. There was almost no traffic on the narrow two-lane road, UNTIL we came nose to nose with a group of stubborn cows who refused to get out of the road.

We blew the horn. We got out and "shooed." Nothing, and there was not enough room to go around them. So, we turned the engine off and ate our picnic lunch. They finally ambled off. I suspect they were grumbling, "Crazy tourists."

That evening, near Hana, we parked the car and walked out to a deserted black sand beach in search of shell treasures. As the sun sank into the sea, the whales came out to play, entertaining us with their joyful antics until all the light was gone from the sky.

Maui has the dubious distinction of being Captain James Cook's landing place, triggering the descent of missionaries and whalers on the islands, resulting in devastation to the native population. In contrast, it also has the honor of being the final home and resting place of aviator Charles Lindbergh.

Moloka'i, The Friendly Isle

Moloka'i, the birthplace of the hula, is the least populated of the islands.

It's tranquility today makes it hard to envision a time in the 1800's when an area of the island, Kalaupapa, became a dumping place for victims of Hansen's Disease (Leprosy). People from all the islands who were suffering from the disease were brought close to shore in boats and thrown into the water. Those who survived, faced pain and hunger in the harshest of wilderness

conditions. A Catholic priest, Father Damian, worked in the colony for sixteen years, until he, too, died from the disease. It was many years before a cure was found for Leprosy and the colony's survivors were allowed to leave the island.

Kalaupapa was declared a National Historic Park in 1980. It is accessible now by foot or mule ride. Don said, "Let's do the mule trip down the mountain." I said, "Not trusting my life to a mule." I won that one.

Instead, we rented a jeep and drove the thirty-six miles across the island, ate interesting food, shopped, and stayed in a great cottage on the beach. Beats mules any day!

Brought home some unique masks, crafted in Bali. Don had fun with them at Halloween, frightening all the trick or treaters.

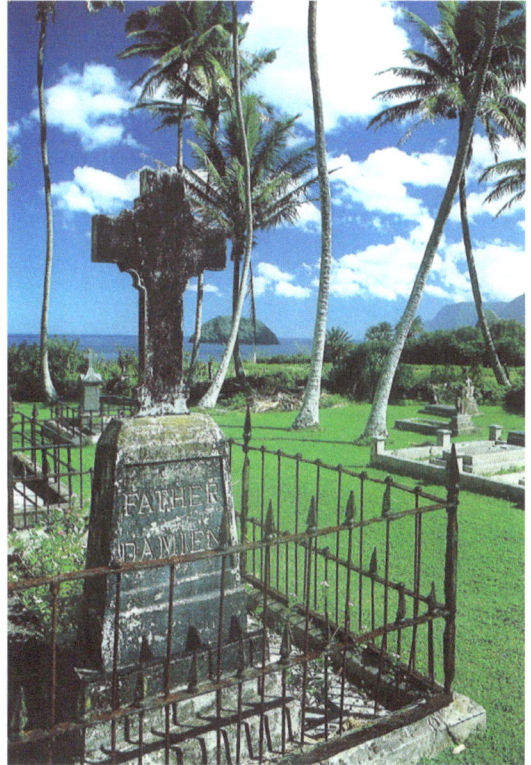

Hawaii, The Orchid Isle

Hawaii, the Big Island, is twice the size of all the other Hawaiian Islands combined and still growing. Lava from active volcanoes constantly adds new territory as it creates incredible black sand beaches. There are vast contrasts in terrain, from mountains to rolling farm land.

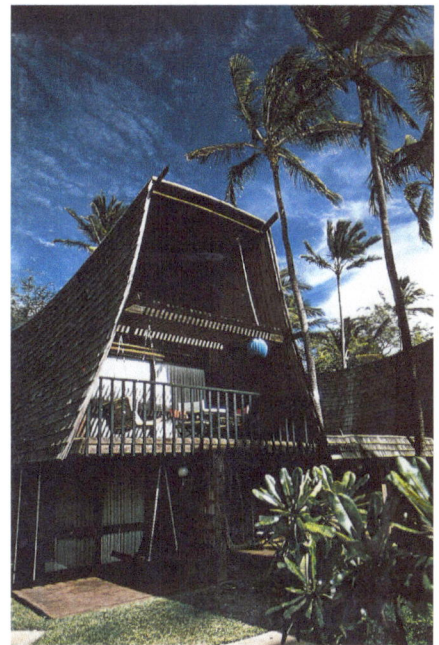

Hilo, the government center, is also the orchid capital of Hawaii and has a funky charm that makes you want to sit down, have a cup of coffee, and gossip with the locals. Up the coast, Waimea is a cow town, boasting the largest cattle ranch in the United States.

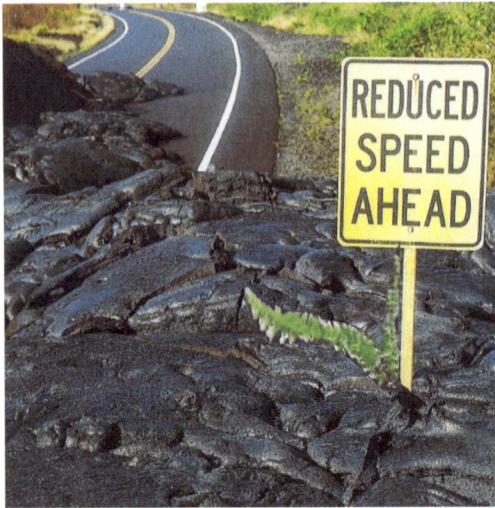

Kona is a fishing village that fulfilled all of our romantic images of the South Seas. We stayed in a charming little bed and breakfast, called the Wild Ginger. I must confess we carried home a few volcanic rocks, complete with fern imprints. They still decorate my foyer at home. The charge to transport the rocks was more than the hotel bill at the Wild Ginger, but worth every penny.

Near Kona is "City of Refuge," a 16th century sanctuary for defeated warriors, ringed by a 1,000 ft. lava wall. Once there, the warrior could be blessed by a Kahuna and return safely to society. It is one of Hawaii's sacred places. When we drove up to Kilauea to pay our respects to Pele, the goddess of the volcano, we were lucky enough to get reservations at the military recreation complex there. There are several tiny houses, beautifully furnished, complete with kitchen, etc., located on the very top of the volcano. It was a unique place to stay, again, thanks to Colonel Don.

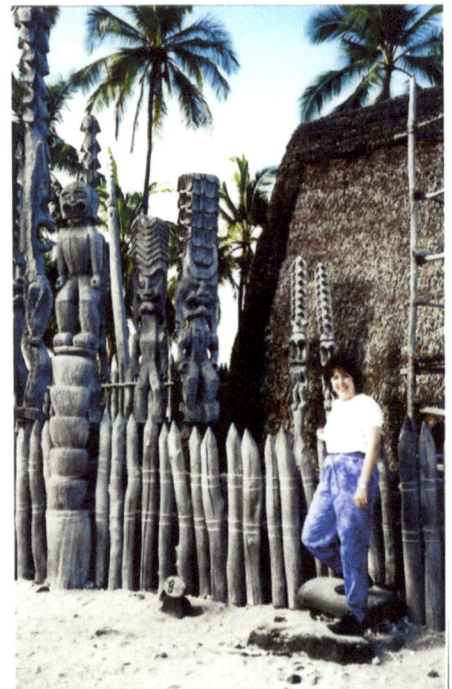

We saw some curious sights besides the obvious ones of boiling lava in the crater and hardened lava every place else, as far as the eye could see. Don kept taking pictures of the amazing patterns in the lava and the little shoots of green peeping up. There are small steaming openings around the outside of the crater, complete with "Do not touch, walk near, etc.," signs. Incredibly, we saw a Japanese family huddled over one of the openings, heating lunch. We pointed to the signs. They smiled and bowed and went right on with lunch.

I cried the day we boarded our homeward bound plane, florist boxes clutched under our arms. The Islands of Aloha were the best birthday present ever!

Chapter 6

Road Trip

A Love Letter to America

Westward Ho!

When we returned from our amazing, wonderful, never-want-to-go-home trip to Hawaii, Don decided we either had to do some serious work on our faithful motor home or consider trading it in for a newer model. Someone must have been listening because we got a call the next day from a friend who had decided to sell his Winnebago. It was the same length as ours, 22 feet, but was arranged differently, with a real bed in the back, a bigger shower and a table in the kitchen that was just used for A TABLE! There was also a sofa/hide-a-bed in the front so we could take a grandkid along on our adventures if we wished. We looked at each other with wanderlust in our eyes and said, "Done!"

Over the years, we did lots of cross-country trips, some by plane and rental car if our time was short; some in our own car; some in the van; and some in the motor homes. On each trip, we tried to go different routes, see different things. We continued to avoid a hard and fast itinerary. We did detours and turn-arounds. It once took us a week and a half, just to drive down the Oregon Coast because we stopped so often for oohs and aahs and photo ops.

Don's avocation was photography so he never saw a piece of scenery he didn't want to photograph. In one of our scrapbooks, I have a photo of him, on his knees, back to me, hanging over the edge of a canyon, camera in hand. I'm behind him, unseen in the photo, ready to grab his shirttail if he started off the edge! We were a good travel team – he took the photos; I wrote the stories. We were proud that some of our better efforts were published in magazines and journals.

The stories that follow are just a few of our many adventures in the West and Southwest.

Tornado Watch In Oklahoma

The sky grew alarmingly dark and the wind picked up. Our weather radio crackled and popped, warning of hail, heavy rain and damaging winds. A tornado had been spotted twenty miles south of our RV park and was moving in our direction. We were in the middle of nowhere, Oklahoma, with no shelters nearby, and the radio announcer was warning people to avoid the interstate, which was already flooding. There was nothing to do but wait out the storm.

Unconcerned, Don crawled into bed, blankets over his head and went to sleep. How can he do that? Guess that makes me self-appointed storm watcher. Somebody has to do it.

The rain began with a light patter and built quickly to a pounding crescendo. Lightning danced across the night sky, darting close, backing off, circling around us, playing with us.

Thunder crashes shook the ground beneath us. I wondered where the ducks had gone who were begging outside our door a few minutes earlier. I hoped they were high and dry.

Then the wind joined the orchestra of storm sounds, huffing, puffing and rocking our home on wheels from side to side as if it weighed nothing. I sat on the edge of the bed, jacket and purse within reach, poised to wake Don and run, though I didn't know where. I remembered hearing something on the radio about leaving your vehicle and hiding in a ditch. I tried to remember if I'd seen any ditches in the RV park. Don snored on.

For over an hour, the elements battled and I waited for the freight train sound that signals a tornado. Periodically, I checked the windows for leaks and added prized items to my escape bundle. Don never moved. I actually began to hate him a little for sleeping peacefully while the world blew away around us. He should be up, worrying, like I was.

Then, as quickly as it started, the rain and wind and thunder stopped and an eery silence settled over the night. I finally exhaled and dozed, fully clothed, shoes and all, with my escape bundle clutched tightly in my arms, vowing to get even with Don in the morning.

A Man And His Mountain

I went to Crazy Horse Mountain, South Dakota expecting nothing more than a half-finished carving in a rock. I came away from the mountain inspired and humbled by the indomitable spirit of an artist and his family.

A sign greets you as you enter the drive to the information center that stands in the shadow of the memorial. It says, "Never give up your dreams." Boston-born sculptor, Korczak Ziolkowski's dream began in 1939 when he visited the Pine Ridge Reservation and met Chief Henry Standing Bear. The chief asked him to carve a monument to Crazy Horse in the sacred Black Hills that would honor the spirit of the Sioux people.

He told him, "My fellow chiefs and I would like the white man to know the red man has great heroes too." Korczak considered the chiefs' request for seven years before accepting in 1946. It was to be the largest sculptural undertaking in the world – 563 feet high and 641 feet long, carved in the round.

Korczak used his own money to purchase land nearby, promising the chiefs the mountain carving would be the focal point of a vast, non-profit, cultural and educational project. All would be financed through the free enterprise system. He kept his promise. He never took a salary, and twice he turned down $10 million in Federal funding because he felt strongly that the memorial should be financed by the public, not the government which had, time and time again, broken its treaties with the Indians.

Korczak did not like the depiction of the Indian as a defeated and dejected race of people. He designed Crazy Horse as a proud figure, arm outstretched, proclaiming, "My lands are where my dead lie buried."

A three-part memorial plan was designed by Korczak and Chief Henry Standing Bear: the mountain carving, an Indian Museum of North America, and a Medical Training Center and University for the American Indians.

The memorial site was dedicated in 1948, with five of the nine survivors of the Battle of the Big Horn present. Work began in 1949. Korczak had $174 left in his bank account. He lived in a tent in a virtual wilderness for the first seven months, while he built a rough studio/home and roads to get to it. He first worked the mountain under a special use permit, then as a mining claim. In the early 1950s, the Crazy Horse Memorial Foundation acquired the mountain and the 328 acres around it through a land exchange with the Federal Government. Meanwhile, he harvested the trees on his own land and with the help of a volunteer, Ruth Ross, built a 741-step staircase to the summit (6740 ft.). He carried 29 tons of green lumber up the mountain on his back.

Working alone, Korczak spent the first year blasting out the deep cut in front of Crazy Horse's head. His tools were a small jackhammer and an ancient gasoline-fueled compressor. He improvised a creaky cable car to carry his equipment and dynamite.

In 1950, at the age of 40, Korczak married Ruth Ross. They would have ten children together, one of whom he delivered himself when the doctor could not get there in time. The memorial became a family project. The five boys grew up working on the mountain. The five girls helped Ruth with the expanding visitor complex. Everyone worked on the dairy farm and the lumber mill which supported the family and the project.

Chief Henry Standing Bear died in 1943. Korczak was determined to keep his promise to the old man. The work became more dangerous and there were accidents, including a serious back injury that occurred when a cable snapped. The sculptor would undergo four spinal operations between 1961 and 1980. In 1968, he suffered a slight heart attack and in 1969, a massive attack. By this time, 3,200,000 tons of granite had been removed. Korczak continued to do most of the work himself, revising his studio model as the quality of the stone on the mountain dictated.

The Visitor Center began to draw tourists. The Indian Museum was dedicated in 1972. Admission was $4 a carload. The project was out of debt for the first time.

By 1973, Korczak's diabetes and arthritis were worsening. He began to work on his tomb, about 500 yds. from the base of the mountain. Injuries continued. In 1975, his bulldozer cartwheeled 250 ft. down the mountain. He required surgery, but went right back to work, operating the bulldozer in a foot cast.

In July of 1982, Korczak underwent a quadruple heart bypass. He died on Oct. 20, 1982, at the age of 84, and was laid to rest in the tomb near the mountain. The inscription reads, "Korczak, Storyteller in Stone, May His Remains Be Left Unknown." He had labored 33 years on the mountain, yet the face of Crazy Horse was barely discernable.

Korczak's dream didn't end with his death. He knew completion of the monument would require more than one lifetime. He left scale models, and three books of comprehensive plans and measurements with Ruth and his children. His parting words to his wife were, "You must work on the mountain, but go slowly so you do it right."

Korczak's family is dedicated to carrying on his work and bringing Chief Henry Standing Bear's dream to fruition. The chiseled face of Crazy Horse with its piercing, lifelike eyes, looms 90 ft. on the top of the mountain. The rough-cut of the 262-foot-long arm is outstretched. White paint indicates where the 319-foot-high horse's head will be. Even uncompleted, the work is awesome. The grandeur of the completed memorial can be seen in the scale model.

Thanks to donations from philanthropist, T. Denny Sanford, in 2007, the memorial is now the centerpiece of an educational/cultural center, as Korczak wished. It includes a satellite summer program through the University of South Dakota, called the Indian University of North America, opened in 2010. Its purpose is to validate and empower high school graduates from across the country to aspire to a college education. Scholarships are awarded to those who cannot afford to attend. The summer program is the equivalent of their first semester of college work.

As I left the Crazy Horse campus, the words on the welcome sign took on added meaning. I remembered a letter written by Ruth in 1998 on the 50th anniversary of the project. She wrote, "If you know what you want to do, are willing to work hard enough and pay the price, you can accomplish anything you want in this world."

I drove away, feeling fortunate to have walked on this sacred ground.

Grand Night Out

It was billed as a *Local's Buffet* at the Grand Hotel in Jerome, Arizona. It looked more like a gathering of eclectic movie extras.

Even the setting was larger than life. The three-story Grand Hotel is perched on the side of Cleopatra Hill, 5,000 feet up, tucked into the rocky hillside of what once was the richest copper mining town in America. During its 70-year life, the Gold King Mine produced a billion-dollars-worth of copper, gold and silver.

The hotel building is massive, constructed of steel and concrete to withstand the winds and resist the ravages of the fire-prone desert. It is rumored, the ghosts of the men who toiled in the mountain mines walk the dark halls after midnight. The building originally housed the hospital that cared for the 3,000+ miners. Imagine the stories those walls could tell.

As we entered the dining room, I was struck by the timelessness of the simple wooden tables and chairs, the massive, carved wooden bar. Wyatt Earp and Wild Bill Hickok would have been right at home here. Before the evening was over, I had seen several of their look-a-likes.

I sat down at one of the small wooden tables, gritty with sand carried in by the wind through the open double doors. It was sundown. The view from the dining room balcony was a rosy delight, making the gritty table less important in the overall scheme of things.

The buffet was good home cooking, plus all the jalapenos that could be found in the city of Jerome. They were in everything--the macaroni and cheese, the bread, the chicken. My mouth burned for hours. The mashed potatoes had somehow escaped, so I ate lots of those, hoping they would absorb the fire. The food didn't matter all that much. My focus was on the characters around me.

There were cowboys with scuffed boots and dusty hats. And no, they did not remove their hats in the dining room. Must be a different set of rules in the Wild West.

There were lots of *good ole boy* types, the kind you know drive rusty pick-up trucks with hounds in the back and shotguns displayed proudly in the rear window.

A table of tourists in brightly flowered Hawaiian shirts kept asking if the air conditioning was broken and complaining because there was no fat-free salad dressing on the salad bar.

Seated at the table behind us was a group of five women, probably in their forties, casually but classically dressed, carrying on what appeared to be serious conversations in the din of animated voices and boisterous background music. They were probably school teachers out for an evening on the town but my imagination was working overtime. So I decided they must be a Western "Kensington Ladies Society," doing research for their next erotic book.

At a small table against the wall, two young men with bleached, spikey hair and lots of intriguing body piercings were sketching the people in the room. I wondered if they would try to market their art to the diners but they didn't. They just kept sketching.

There were several Grandma and Grandpa types with deeply wrinkled farm faces, enjoying dinner out with their children and grandchildren.

The teens and twenty-somethings were in tight jeans and tank tops, laughing and flirting around the bar.

The largest group of characters were the hippies. They looked to be in their forties or fifties but were still lost in that era of long hair and beards for men, and long, shapeless, tie-dyed dresses on the women. They blended into the mix, just like everyone else. Looking around the room, I felt caught up in a time warp, where I was the one out of place. It was an open mic night. The first entertainers were Simon and Garfunkel wannabes who sang familiar songs that carried me back to a time when bare feet and pony tails were the order of the day. The two entertainers had both.

It was easy to get lost in the revelry and forget that I am a responsible mother of two grown children. Just for a few moments, it was fun to pretend to be young and free. It was not difficult to understand why these lost flower children may have chosen to remain lost. What, after all, are they missing--stressful jobs in crowded, polluted cities, wearing uncomfortable shoes and stifling neckties. Maybe, they are the smart ones and WE are the lost souls.

Panic in the Grand Canyon

The Grand Canyon was Don's "happy place," – a favorite destination for hiking and photography. It was not mine because of my fear of heights. But it is true that exposure to the things you fear, sometimes lessens that fear. I was determined to learn to love those steep cliffs and rocky trails.

We traveled to both the North and South Rims in every season of the year. I love the North Rim in late spring when blossoms peep from beneath that last layer of melting snow and the sun feels delicious on your shoulders. It also is less traveled than the South Rim, particularly at that time of year, and it's easier to get reservations at El Tovar, the historic lodge, perched on the edge of the canyon. The South Rim has lots of short, protected trails with rock barriers that allow novice hikers and children to enjoy the splendor of the canyon without risk. Autumn in both the North and South Rims is spectacular. Winter snow transforms the canyon into a wonderland.

Don liked to get off the more touristy trails and search for unusual views for his photos. One day on the North Rim, we followed a wooded trail, well-marked but not heavily traveled, that took us uphill through thick forest. After hiking for about an hour, the trail emerged from the woods and I was standing on the edge of a sheer cliff, looking down into nothingness. Don kept moving along the narrow path on the rim of the canyon, but I was frozen, terrified. I tried to call out to him to come back or wait for me but my voice was frozen too. Unaware of my plight, he kept walking and was quickly out of sight.

I could feel my heart pounding in my throat. My legs started to tremble. I backed up a few steps to the shelter of the trees and sank to the ground. I tried again to call out and my voice came out a whimper. What to do? I knew he would keep moving till he found that perfect photo spot and probably wouldn't realize until then that I wasn't behind him. I didn't walk as fast as he did so I was always a little behind. He wouldn't think it unusual that I wasn't there. I had a couple of choices. I knew I could not make myself follow that narrow path along the unprotected rim. That was out. I could sit and wait, assuming he would come back and find me. Or I could hike back the way we came, hoping I wouldn't miss the trail markings and become lost. It was late afternoon. It wouldn't be dark for a couple of hours. The hike up the mountain had only taken an hour. I decided to wait.

It was quiet and I jumped at every rustling sound. I pulled out my water bottle and panicked anew when I realized it was only half full. Don had the snacks and extra water in his backpack. I told myself I was just being silly. Of course, he would come back for me. But, that scared voice inside my head argued, he had no way of knowing when or where I stopped. What if the trail took him down the mountain a different way? How would he explain to my children that he'd lost their mother in the wilds of Arizona? After a half hour of catastrophizing and wondering if there were bears in the woods, I heard voices coming up the trail. A young couple emerged from the woods. I explained my predicament. They promised to run ahead and find Don. I explained, "He will be the one with the camera, hanging over the edge of the canyon."

That's exactly how they found him, totally preoccupied with the view and unaware of my panic. He figured I was dawdling along, picking wildflowers, as I like to do, or resting on a rock a few yards back. Rescued and feeling a little foolish, I led the way back down the hill, determined not to be left behind again.

Sharon Canfield Dorsey

DINOSAUR NAT. PK.
reminds us that no matter
how big you are, Mother
Nature can take you out.

These bones are from
a medium-sized dinosaur.

Once the bed of an
ancient river, later tilted
by earthquakes, this thin
sandstone layer has
yielded thousands of
fossil bones which were
uncovered and left in
the mountain.

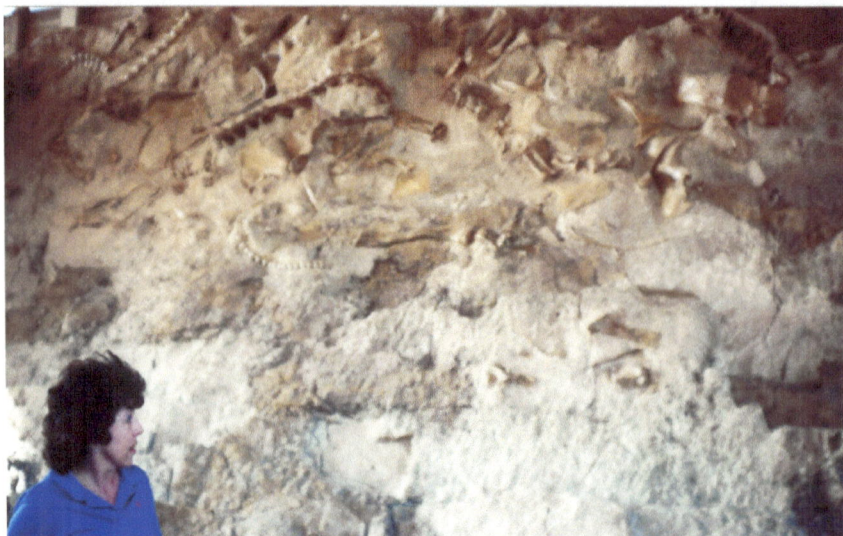

62

Chapter 7

Road Trip

A Love Letter to America

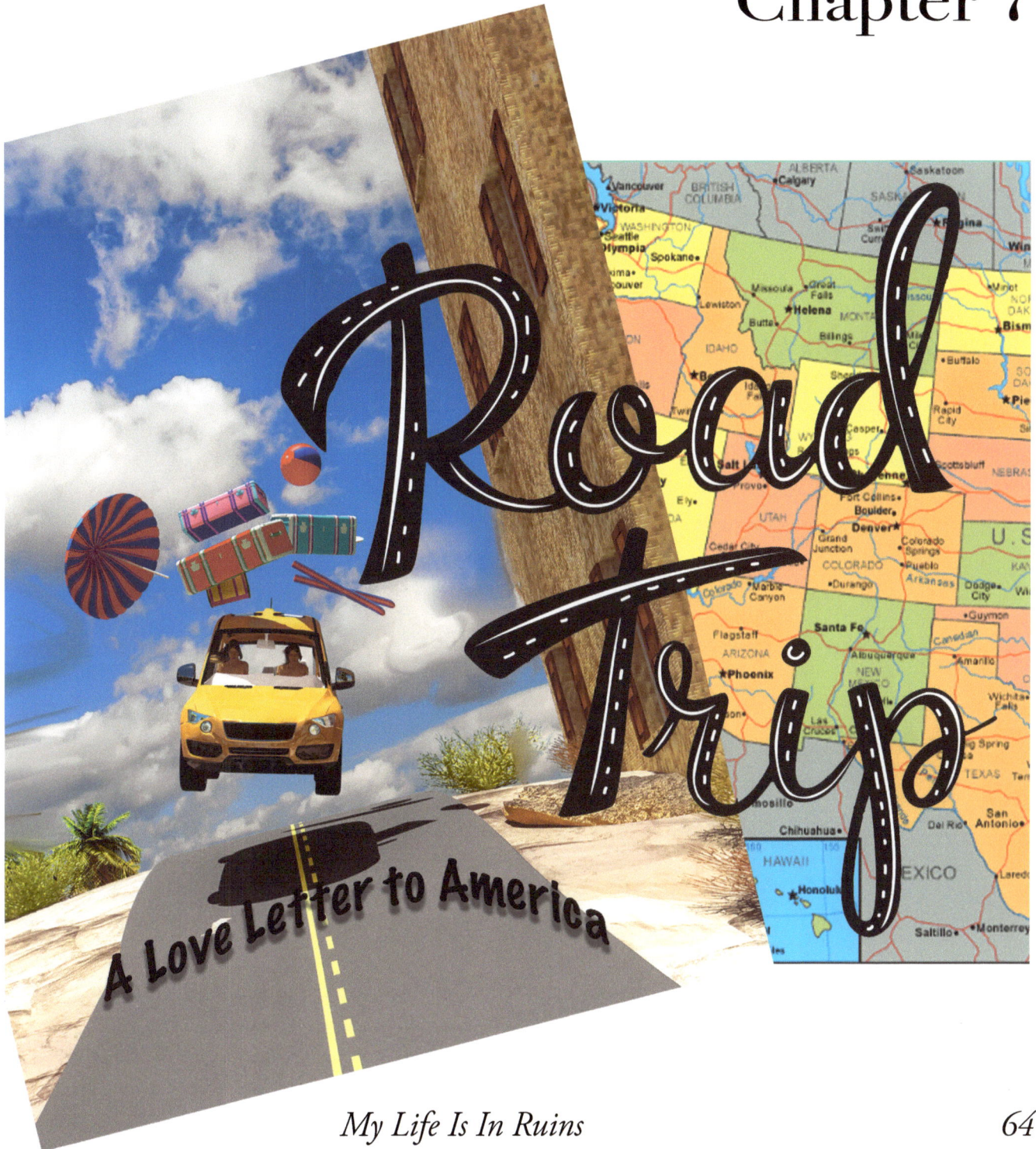

My Life Is In Ruins

In the depths of the human spirit is a desire to trace the paths of our ancestors. These journeys are food for the soul. I have a sweatshirt that proclaims, "My life is in ruins." For many of us descended from Native Americans, our past truly is in the ruins left behind by earlier generations, going all the way back to the Clovis People, believed to be predecessors of most indigenous cultures in America including the Anasazi, or Ancient Ones. The Anasazi left behind carvings on rock, pottery, woven baskets and magnificent structures built into the mountains. We wanted to visit as many of those sacred places as we could.

Mesa Verde – (550 – 1270 Ce)

MESA VERDE NATIONAL PARK

Around 2,000 years ago, a creative, industrious people inhabited the high, green table plateau of Southwestern Colorado. They built multi-storied dwellings into the overhanging cliffs, 2,000 ft. above, and farmed the plateau below. These settlements once supported 7,000 people. Imagine a collection of apartment buildings with 7,000 residents!

Research indicates the people began abandoning their clifftop homes around the year 1200 and migrating south. No one knows for sure why, but a long-term drought is a possibility. It is believed modern-day Pueblo, Zuni and Hopi tribes descended from the Anasazi.

Today Mesa Verde is a World Heritage Site. Over 3,900 sites have been located within the 52,000 acres of the park and 600 of them are cliff-dwellings. As we climbed the crude stairs dug into the rock, tiptoed carefully through the Cliff Palace and Spruce Tree dwellings, saw the carvings and pot shards left behind, this visitor felt humbled to be able to walk in the footsteps of the Ancient Ones.

Tuzigoot And Palatki, (Near Sedona, Arizona)...

The Red Rock country of Sedona is one of my favorite areas in the Southwest. It is incredibly beautiful, spiritual AND houses more art galleries than anyplace we've visited. A shopper's delight!

In the Verde Valley Region of Sedona, we visited several prehistoric Indian settlements of the Sinagua people, (1150CE – 1400's), sometimes referred to as the "people in between." The Verde Valley became a human melting pot of cultures – influenced by the Anasazi; the Magollons; and the Hohokam people. Tuzigoot is a magnificent hillside pueblo, two stories high with seventy-seven rooms. We were surprised to see no exterior doors. We entered the rooms by way of ladders through the roof.

Nearby is the sister pueblo of Palatki, consisting of two large buildings, built at the base of a sheer cliff in a box canyon. The Sinaguas were traders. Among the things found on-site were parrot feathers from Mexico and fine jewelry featuring turquoise and seashells from California. The site was abandoned in the 1400's, perhaps for the same reason the Anasazi left their homes – a continuing drought. The nearby RED CLIFFS shelter an impressive rock art collection of pictographs and petroglyphs, left there by several native cultures. A pictograph is an illustration painted or applied to a surface. A petroglyph is scratched or scraped onto a surface. Think of them as prehistoric newspapers. Newspaper Rock in Utah is a great example.

Wupatki And Sunset Crater (Near Flagstaff, Arizona)...

On our way to the Grand Canyon, we decided to stop at Sunset Crater. In 1064CE, a volcano erupted, setting into motion a 200-year volcanic tantrum that resulted in Sunset Crater. The cinders formed a kind of mulch, holding in moisture, ideal for growing crops. Give the people land for growing crops and they will come. They did and built the Wupatki dwellings. This multi-story dwelling had more than a hundred rooms and probably housed 150 people at its peak.

The residents were an assortment of Anasazi, Magollan and Hohokam, working together to survive in that dry climate for about 150 years. They deserted the site when the volcano became dormant. They were collectively called the Hisatsinom and are claimed by the Hopi as their ancestors.

We discovered this site contains a blowhole or "breathing cave." A blowhole is an opening in the earth where water-cooled air rushes out when air pressure underground is greater than above ground. It was considered sacred by the Indians. We might consider it "nature's air conditioning."

Sky City, Acoma Pueblo, (60 Miles West Of Albuquerque, New Mexico)

Sky City is the oldest continuously inhabited city in the country, dating from 1075. The city was built atop a great sandstone rock, 400 feet high. There are about 600 residents, no water or electricity. Homes continue to be handed down, generation to generation, on the mother's side. It is a matriarchal society and women are much respected and, according to our guide, much feared. Men own nothing and have no monetary control.

Our guide was a funny little man, named Orlando, who shared Sky City history with great touches of dry humor. Visitors cannot enter the village without a guide and a paid fee. He walked around with us and told us gruesome stories of the slavery and cruelty in the era of Spanish/Catholic domination. The residents had tables set up in front of their houses and after the tour, we were invited to go back around with another guide, after paying another fee, to shop. I think it's called, "getting even with the white man," and in my opinion, well-deserved. We were happy to pay the fees.

Acoma is world-famous for its stunning black and white pottery. It was fun to select special pieces from the resident artists. To our surprise, we were invited inside one of the homes by a lovely woman who served us Blue Corn Bread (delicious). It was ninety degrees outside but cool and comfortable inside the pueblo walls. To my surprise, the furnishings looked much like the ones I grew up with in the 50's, complete with crocheted doilies on the tables.

Our home for the night was Red Rock State Park, near Gallup, N. M. To our delight, the Acoma Dancers were the entertainers for the evening. The only thing rivaling their performance that night was the thrill of being in the portable "john" by the railroad tracks when the Atchison, Topeka and Santa Fe train came roaring through. I thought for sure Armegeddon had come.

Kokopelli

During our many travels through the Four Corners area, where the states of Arizona, Colorado, New Mexico, and Utah intersect, we were constantly seeing references to or drawings of Kokopelli, a hunchbacked figure in various postures, playing a flute. Some called him the Trickster. Some called him a clown. He has come to be known as the Casanova of the Ancient Ones. The name Kokopelli derives from the northwestern Arizona Hopi people who have a kachina god named after the flute player. Over time, the image of the traveling minstrel spread far beyond his original Four Corners homeland, turning up three thousand miles away in Eastern Canada in the Peterborough Petroglyphs, begging the question of how and when the Hopi traveled that far.

Sacred Places...

The Southwest is full of sites that are sacred to native people. Canyon de Chelly and Monument Valley in Arizona are spectacular, as are Chaco Canyon and Shiprock in New Mexico. Zion and Bryce National Parks in Utah are just as beautiful covered with snow in the winter as they are in summer's tourist season. Canyonlands is a wonderland of natural rock sculptures. Sadly, many sacred sites are being threatened by timbering, fracking, and greed.

Best Ever Family Reunion

They gather on the National Mall in Washington, D. C.,
twenty-five thousand strong,
indigenous people from throughout the Western Hemisphere,
representing four hundred twenty tribes,
in full buckskin, beads, and feather regalia, to honor and celebrate
the opening of the National Museum of the American Indian.

A wrinkled Cherokee grandmother tells me,
"The spirits of the ancestors march with us today,
the spirits of the sixty-three million native people,
murdered to make way for civilization."
I believe her, feel their presence,
mourn their pain with my tears.

The Native Nations procession stretches
from the Washington Monument to the museum.
The alphabetical list of tribes fills six pages in the program.
Aztec...Chickahominy... Hopi...Sioux... Zuni...
...twenty-five thousand stand in place under a blazing sun for hours,
drumming, chanting--families with children, ancient ones in wheelchairs.

The end of the procession takes three hours to arrive at the museum.
No matter, the wait or the walk.
The journey to this moment has taken centuries.
At last there is a gathering place to preserve our history,
a permanent campfire
around which our stories will be told.

The spirits of the ancestors will no longer wander in restless silence.
They can rest in peace in this sacred place.

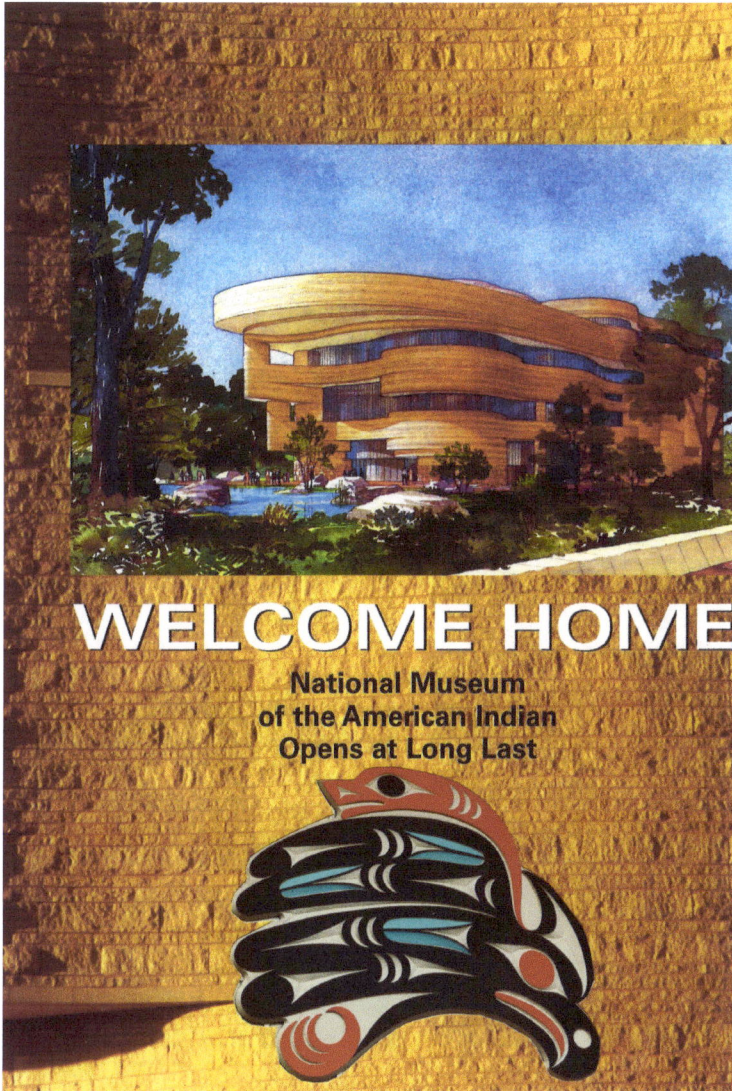

WELCOME HOME

National Museum
of the American Indian
Opens at Long Last

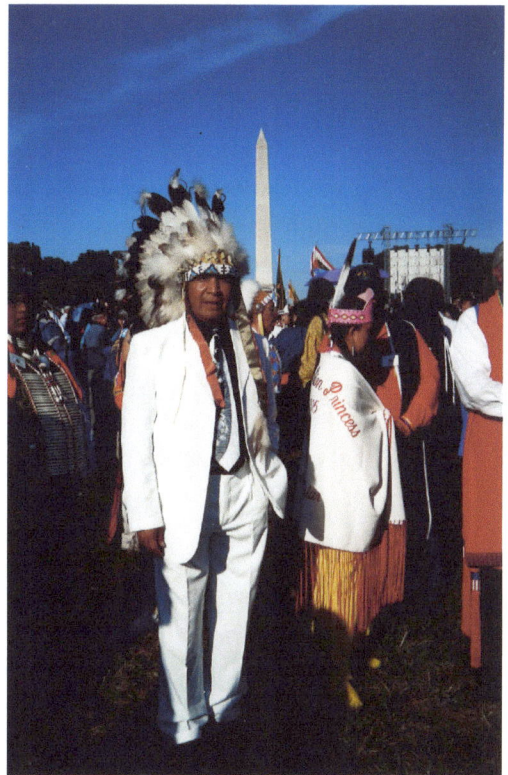

Gold And Corruption
In The Black Hills

Who owns the Black Hills?
Depends on who you ask.
An 1868 treaty says the Sioux and Arapaho people own it.
Why?
Spoils of war won by great Sioux Warrior Chief, Red Cloud.
He defeated the U. S. Army, stopping wagon trains moving into Indian territory.
Negotiations followed. Thirteen tribal nations spoke their truth.
Seven government peace commissioners listened and signed before thirty witnesses.

Peace lasted until 1874, when the U. S. Government seized the land.
Why?
Gold was discovered in the Black Hills of South Dakota and Wyoming.
Thousands of fortune seekers invaded the Sioux lands.
The government offered compensation in 1877.
The Sioux refused, quoting Lakota Chief, Crazy Horse,
"One does not sell the earth upon which the people walk."
The lands guaranteed to them by the U. S. Government were not for sale.

So, who owns the sacred Black Hills?
The Supreme Court ruled in 1980 that the United States had acted in bad faith.
Fair compensation to the tribes was set at $102 million.
The settlement has appreciated to $1.3 billion today, representing
only a fraction of the gold, timber and other resources removed.
The Sioux will not accept any payment. They do not want money.
They want their sacred Black Hills back as promised in the 36-page
Treaty of Fort Laramie, signed May 25, 1868, one hundred fifty one years ago.

The treaty is on exhibit at the Smithsonian National Museum of the American Indian, along with many others dishonored and disregarded by the U.S. government. "It is my wish that the United States honor this treaty," says Chief John Spotted Tail (Sicangu Lakota, citizen of Rosebud Sioux Tribe), great-great-grandson of Spotted Tail, one of the treaty's original signers.

"One does not sell the earth upon which the people walk."

Bear's Ears...It's Not Just Land

Bear's Ears National Monument in Utah is ancestral homeland

to the Hopi, Ute, Zuni Pueblo and the Navajo Nation,

beginning 13,000 years ago with the Clovis people,

predecessors of most indigenous cultures in the Americas.

100,000 archaeological sites of the Pueblo nations are embedded

in the steep cliffs, canyons and mesas of the 1.3 million-acre Monument.

Anasazi bones lie there, dust to dust,

amidst the scraps of baskets, pottery and tools they left behind.

Our government proposes opening 88% of this sacred land

to pipelines, lumbering, and cattle grazing,

once again ignoring the treaties, contracts,

and promises made to native people.

Bear's Ears is not just land.

It is a centuries old burial ground.

Arlington Cemetery is also a burial ground.

Would our government dig a pipeline through Arlington?

EXPLORE ➤

ROOM AT THE TOP...
Hiking in Guardsman's
Pass, Park City, Utah.

ADVICE...Never eat
lunch before riding the
Alpine Slide down the
mountain. (No pics of
that event for obvious
reasons.)

New Mexico

SHIPROCK, on the
Navajo Reservation,
is the hardened lava
of a volcano.
Altitude 7,178
Can be seen for miles
in the desert.

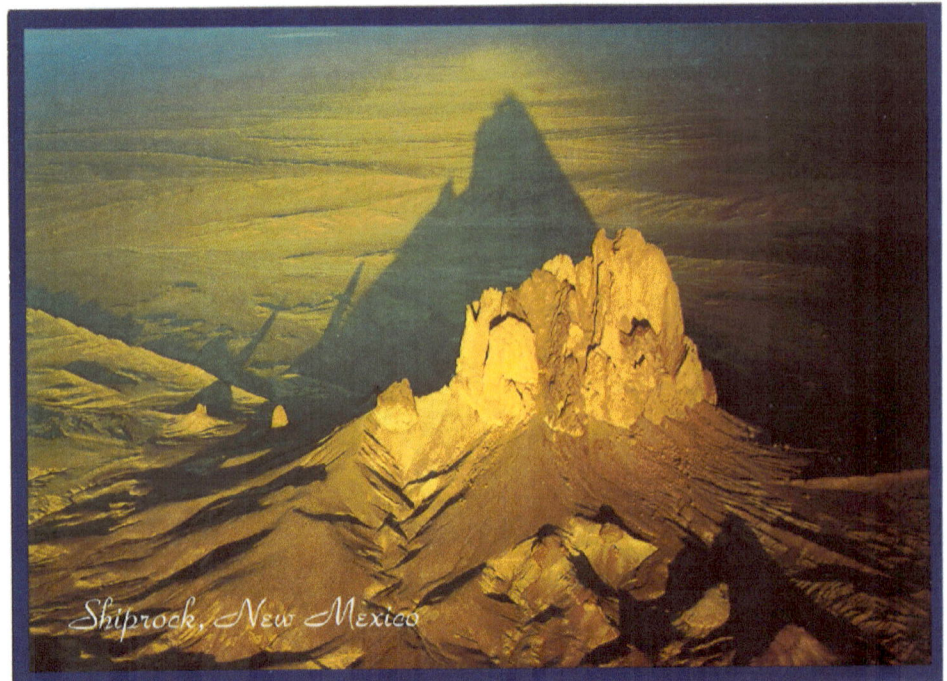

Shiprock, New Mexico

Road Trip

A Love Letter to America

PLACES TO GO,
THINGS TO DO,
LESSONS TO LEARN,
ON YOUR SUMMER
VACATIONS...

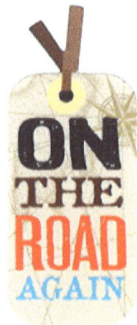

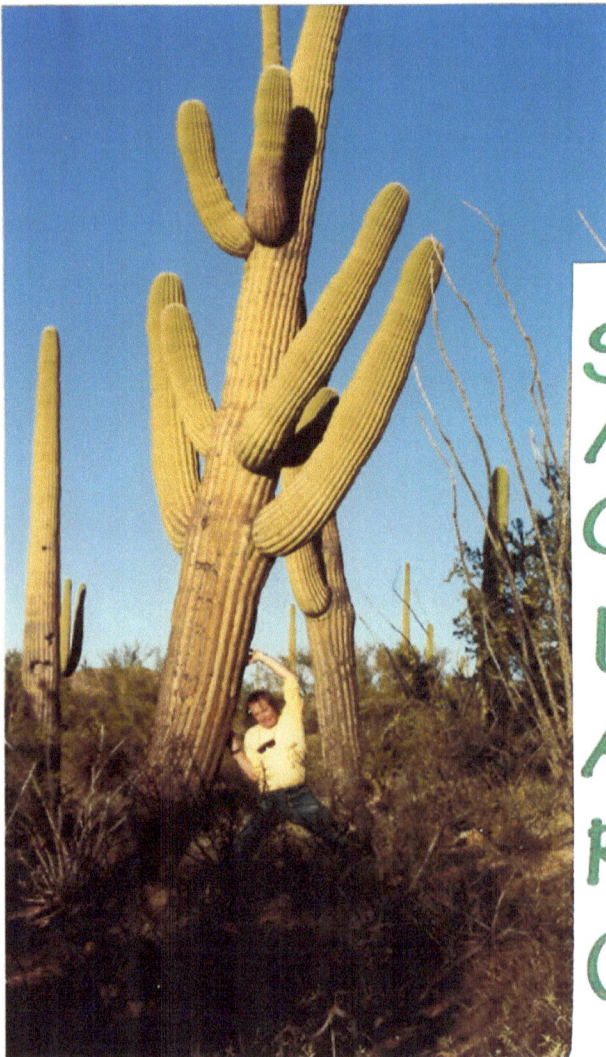

ON
THE
ROAD
AGAIN

AMBER WAVES
OF GRAIN - 22
PURPLE MTN.
MAJESTY - 40

FRUITED PLAIN - 119

SAGUARO

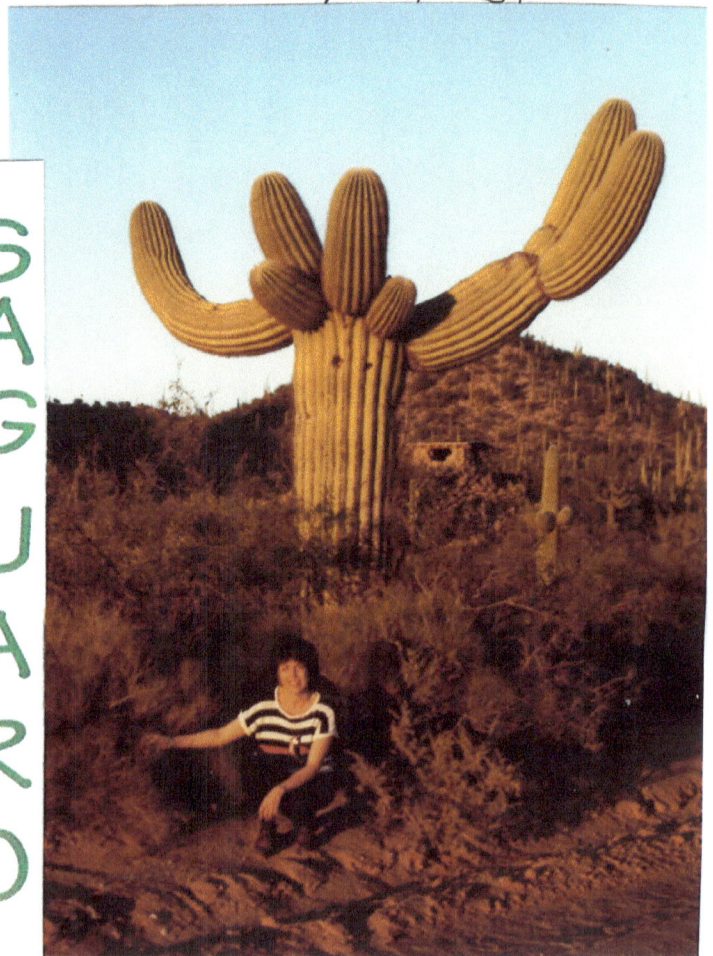

The giant cactus in Arizona are admirable but NOT huggable, like the Redwoods.

Posing with a fat Redwood,
makes you look skinny.

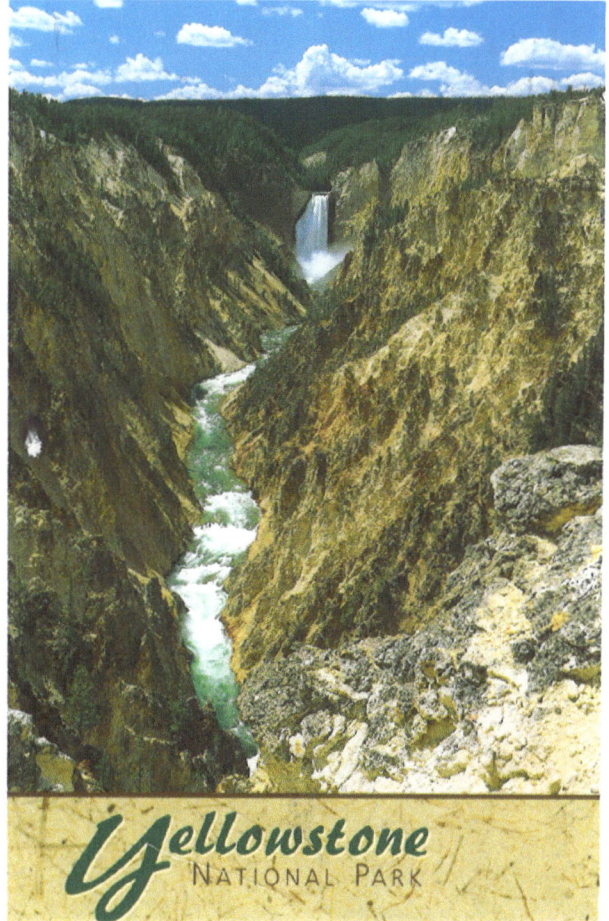

Bad place to lose a cow!

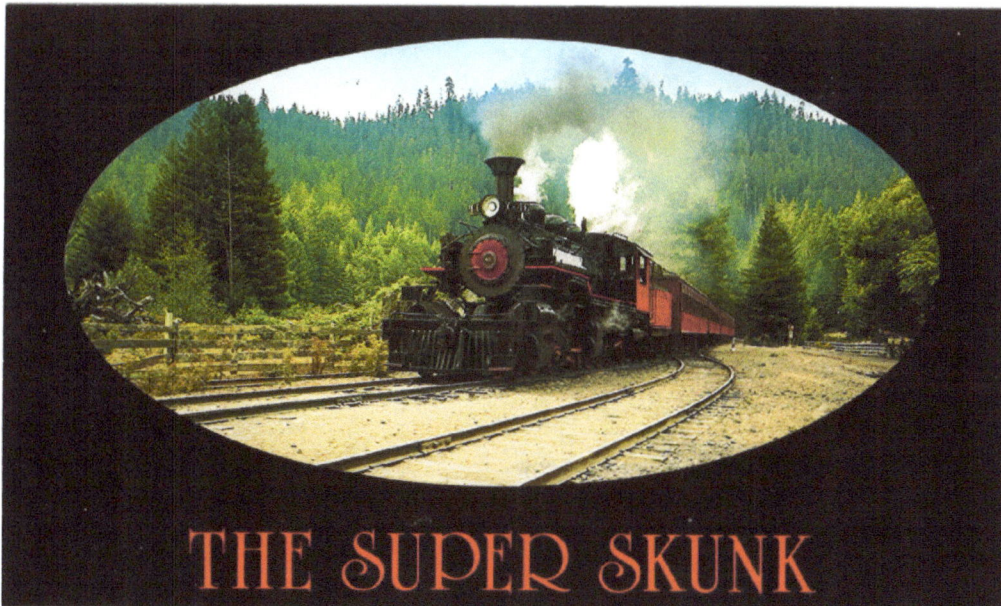

The steam train through the Redwoods really DOES smell like skunk.

PIKES PEAK...Cog train took us from
80 degrees in a flowery meadow to 35 degrees
and snow on the 14,110 peak AND it took us
up the mountain facing BACKWARDS in
order to be able to make the steep, slow climb.
Train doesn't turn around, so we went back down
much faster and facing forward. EXCITING!

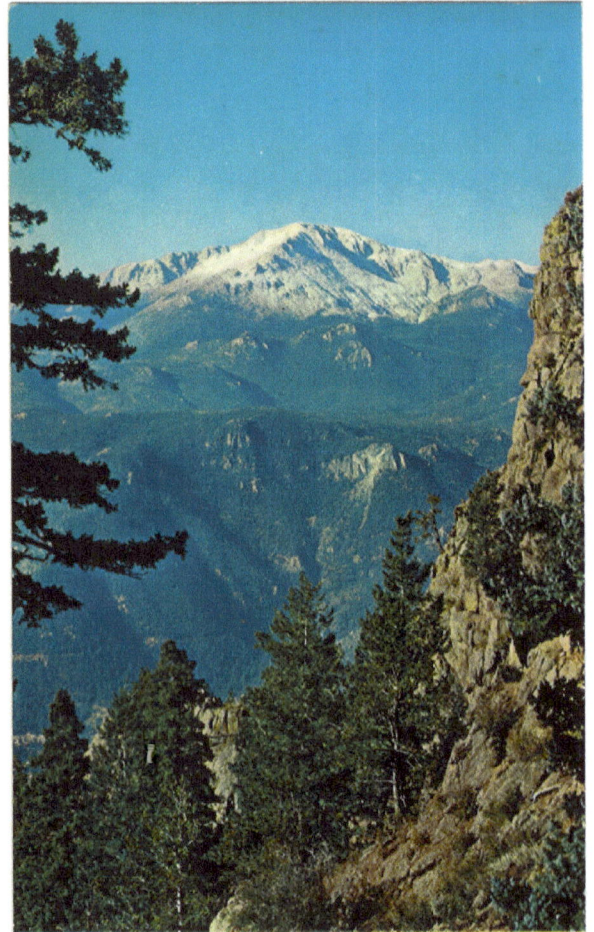

World Famous Pikes Peak, Colorado

COLORADO ADVICE...
Take 2 credit cards if you
go to lunch in Vail, CO.
(No pics of lunch – had to
hock the camera.)

Cog Train on Pikes Peak

Now I understand why Robert Redford never wants to leave his home in Utah.

In the Mormon Tabernacle, in Salt Lake City, Utah, the acoustics are so amazing, you can hear a pin drop from one end of an enormous room to the other. No wonder the Choir sounds so good there.

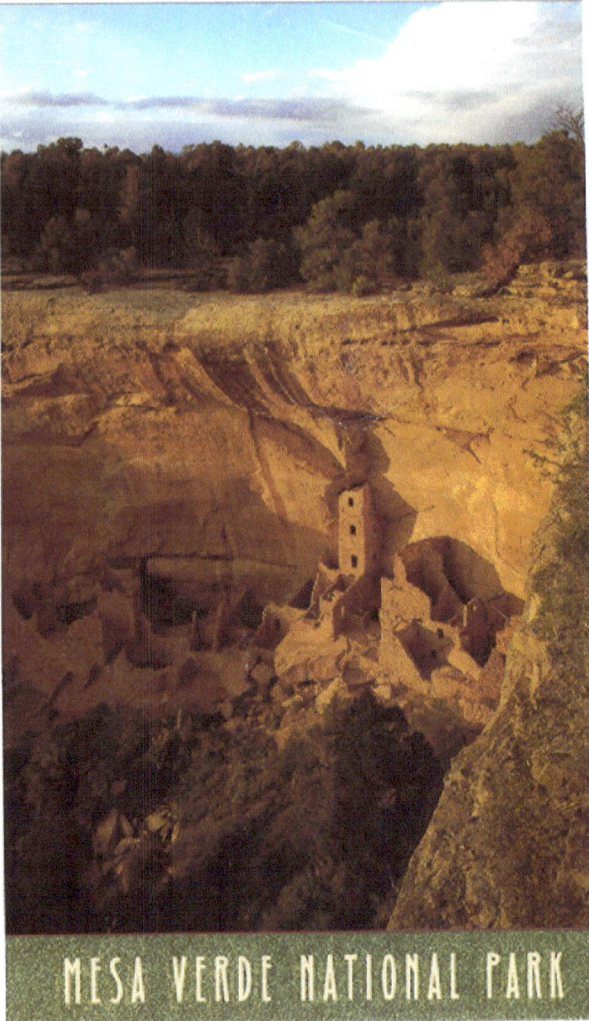

MESA VERDE NATIONAL PARK

Native Americans were building palaces
long before real estate agents were invented.

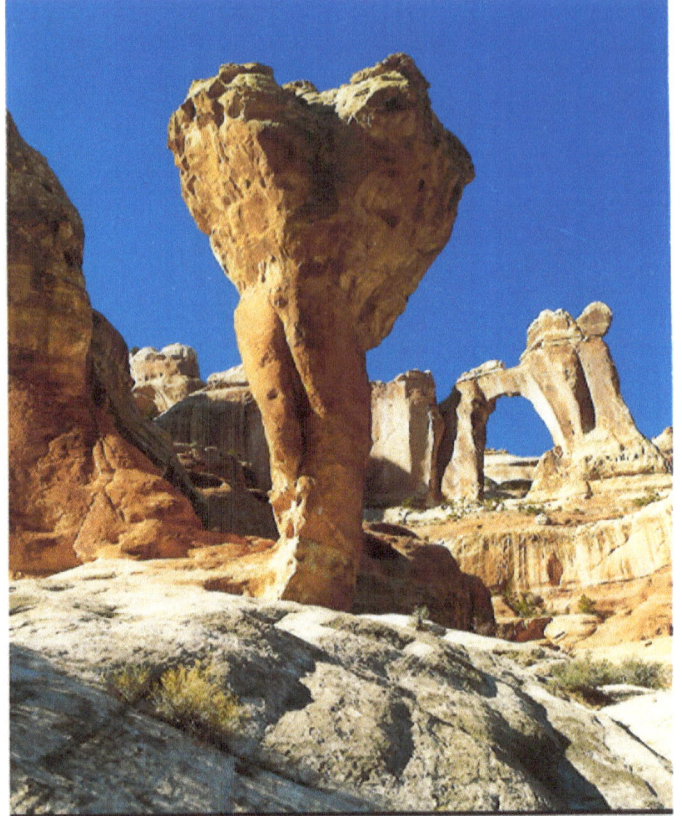

CANYONLANDS
National Park

Can't find carvings like these in museums.

Journalism has been around a long time.

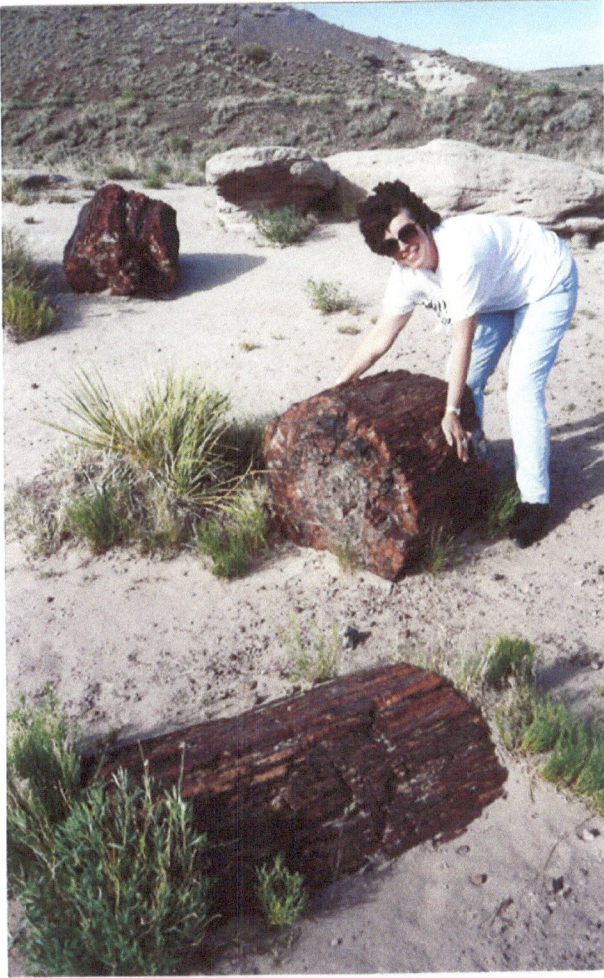

Some places frown on guests carrying off the rocks. (Petrified Forest, AZ)

FISHERS, however, is happy to take your money and load them in the car. Rock Hound Heaven!

DON'T LOOK DOWN!!

Salt Flats in Utah brought
back memories for Don
of racing here in the hotrod
he built in his teens.

I found my thrill!
Wanted to bring it home.

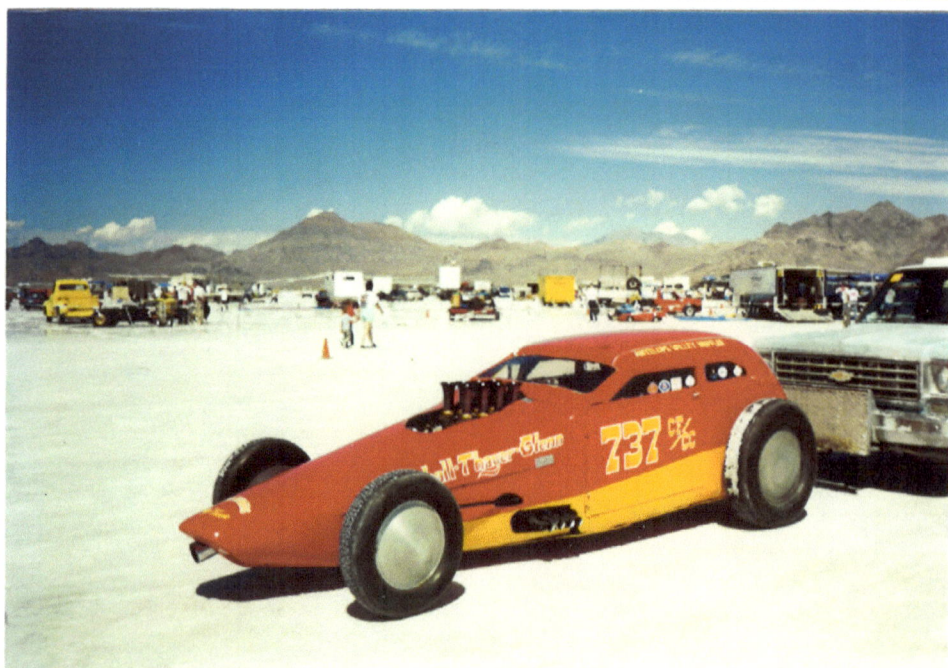

GETTYSBURG breaks your heart. When the Confederate and Union armies marched away from Gettysburg in July, 1863, they left behind 51,000 killed, wounded, and missing soldiers.

More than 3500 Union soldiers are interred at Gettysburg Cemetery. Most Confederate casualties were removed from battlefield graves and reinterred in the South.

12,000 Confederates advanced across open fields in "Pickett's Charge." 5000 men became casualties within an hour.

MY DREAM HOUSE,
FALLINGWATER,
near Ohiopyle State
Park, Pennsylvania,
designed by Frank Lloyd
Wright in 1936, was built
over a cascading waterfall.

Water flows through a part
of the living area and
into the waterfall. The
house was build into and
around huge boulders. Most
of the furniture is built into
the walls.

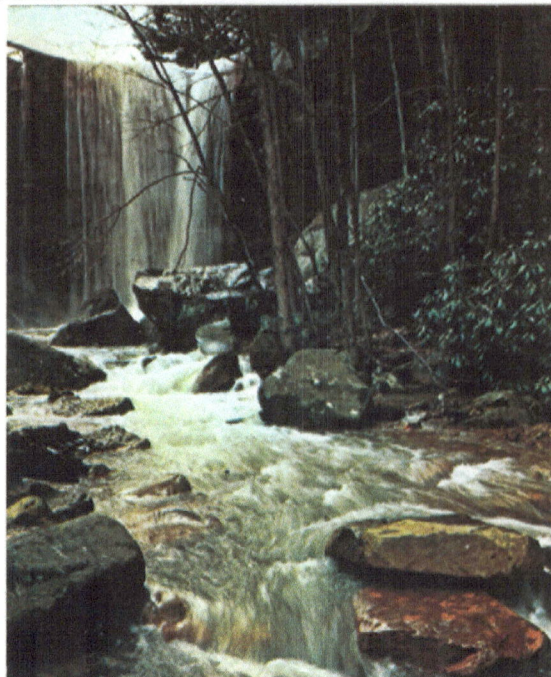

Cucumber Falls at
Ohiopyle St. Pk, PA.
A favorite camping
and kayaking spot of
Don's paddlers and
campfollowers (me).

IN PARK CITY, UTAH, EVEN THE MOOSE SKI (AND WEAR HIGH HEELS)

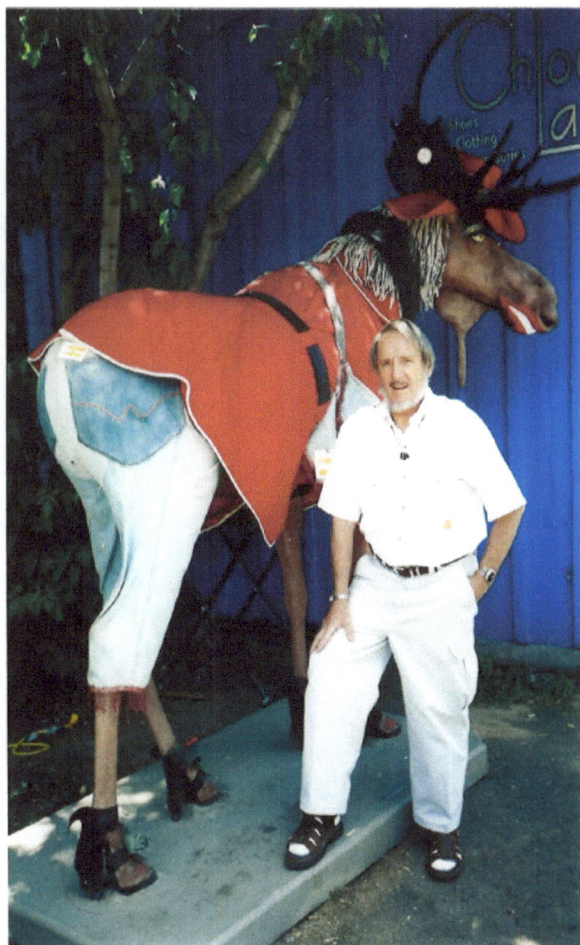

Advice For The Novice Traveler

1. I don't advise tent camping in 102-degree weather. Reserve that for the mountains.

2. If this is your first experience with RVing, rent one and take it to a nearby park for a week-end to try out all the equipment. Better to have a malfunction there than on the road.

3. Don't buy an RV till you've survived and loved your first trip.

4. Pack your RV light. Just because there are closets doesn't mean you have to fill them. Remember, you will need room for the treasures you find along the way.

5. If you are active duty or retired military, there are lots of campgrounds, RV parks, hotels, etc. especially for you and your family. Do your research and take advantage of them.

6. There are designated wilderness areas all across the country that allow free camping. They do not have power hook-ups and some have size limitations for RV's. That's why we always chose a smaller vehicle, to have the flexibility. Some scenic roads also have size limitations.

7. State and National Parks are your friends – beautiful scenery, nice people and cheaper fees than privately operated camping areas.

8. Most campgrounds and RV parks have laundry facilities and small grocery stores for your convenience, although, it never seemed fair to me, that you still have to do laundry on vacation.

9. Carry all medications you will need AND a good First Aid Kit for those unexpected scratches and upset stomachs.

10. Stay in touch with family or friends. Someone should know where you are, especially if you're wilderness camping.

11. Keep a journal. You think you will remember everything you saw and did but you won't, so write it down.

12. If your travel time is short, fly to the area you want to explore and rent a car. You can still see the country – just in small bites. Make a travel wish list and work your way down the list.

13. Talk to people as you're traveling around. We found other campers to be especially friendly and eager to share experiences. They gave us tips about campgrounds, fun places to go, unusual sights. We also found "Mom and Pop" restaurants to be great places to get information about the town AND find great food. People love talking about themselves and their town.

14. Learn everything you can about your destination before you get there. Your research will save you time and money plus reward you with intriguing, little-known sites to explore.

15. Don't be reluctant to travel with children. They are little sponges who will soak up images and experiences. It will be so much easier for them to fall in love with our beautiful country when they've visited its mountains, rivers and deserts. What they love, they will preserve. Preservation of and respect for our land is an important lesson we must teach the next generation. It is, undoubtedly, the most valuable legacy we can leave.

About the Author

SHARON CANFIELD DORSEY has published fiction, non-fiction, juvenile fiction and poetry in magazines, newspapers, journals and anthologies. She is a member of National League of American Pen Women, Inc., James City Poets, Poetry Society of Virginia, The Writers Guild of Virginia, and the Chesapeake Bay Writers.

Sharon has received awards from Christopher Newport University Writer's Conference, Poetry Society of Virginia, Gulf Coast Writer's Association, and Chesapeake Bay Writers. She was a winner of the Art Lit Project, which displayed her poetry on the sidewalks of the city of Williamsburg, VA.

She is author of four children's books, *Herman, the Hermit Crab and the Mystery of the Big, Black, Shiny, Thing; Revolt of the Teacups; Buddy and Ballerina Save the Library; Buddy the Bookworm Rescues the Doomed Books*; a book of poetry, *Tapestry*; and a memoir, *Daughter of the Mountains*. Her poems are also included in an anthology, *Captured Moments*.

Sharon is a Senior Sales Director of 40 years with Mary Kay Cosmetics, Mom to son, Steven and daughter, Shannon, and grandmother to Adaline, Emma and Zachary.

Other Books by Sharon Dorsey

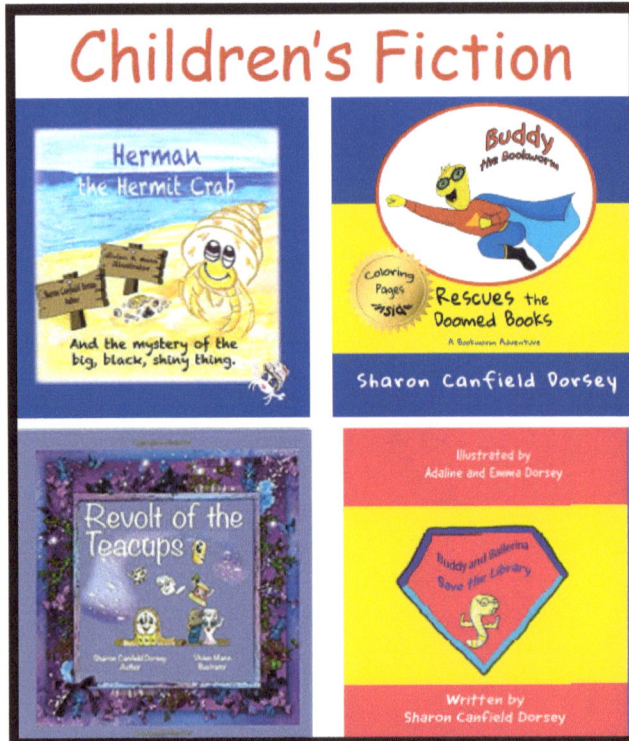

Children's Fiction

Herman the Hermit Crab
And the mystery of the big, black, shiny thing.
Sharon Canfield Dorsey, Author
Vivian Marie, Illustrator

Buddy the Bookworm
Rescues the Doomed Books
A Bookworm Adventure
Coloring Pages Inside
Sharon Canfield Dorsey

Revolt of the Teacups
Sharon Canfield Dorsey, Author
Vivian Marie, Illustrator

Illustrated by
Adaline and Emma Dorsey
Buddy and Ballerina
Save the Library
Written by
Sharon Canfield Dorsey

Sharon Canfield Dorsey
award winning author and poet

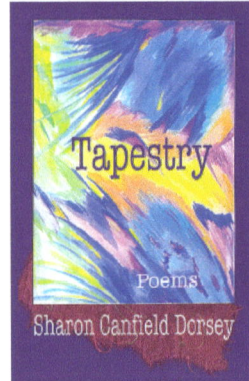

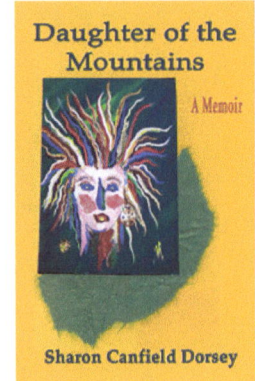

Anthologies

Tapestry
Poems
Sharon Canfield Dorsey

Daughter of the Mountains
A Memoir
Sharon Canfield Dorsey

The James City Poets
Captured Moments
An Anthology

Williamsburg Virginia
The Journal
Poetry | Essays | Fiction

Unbroken and Unbowed

I was harvested from the earth,
borne on the shoulders of
black slaves and beasts,
split and shorn,
beaten by the ravages of
storm and hate,
shored up by love and
prayer,
withered by unfaithfulness
and uncertainty,
burned but never destroyed,
reached my limbs out to encircle,
my countenance is unwavering,
my Faith is unbreakable,
my God never forsakes me,
I endure!

Elizabeth Bowes

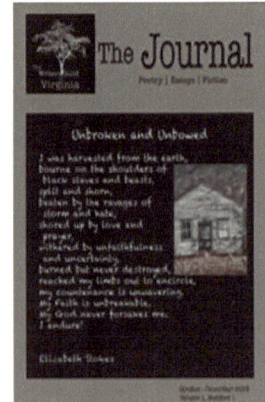

Sharon Dorsey is available for book signings, book talks, seminars and other venues. Please contact her through her website at

www.SharonCanfieldDorsey.com